TONY GRECO

STRONG MIND LEAN BODY

Strategies for Life Success

Foreword by Carol Alt, International Supermodel

THE ULTIMATE PUBLISHING HOUSE (TUPH) US HEADQUARTERS
P.O. Box 1204, Cypress, Texas, U.S.A. 77410

Canadian Office: 205 Glen Shields Avenue, Toronto, Ontario, Canada L4K 2B0
Telephone:647-883-1758

www.ultimatepublishinghouse.com
www. StrongMindLeanBody.com E-mail: info@ultimatepublishinghouse.com

US OFFICE: Ordering Information

Quantity Sales: COMPANIES, ORGANIZATIONS, INSTITUTIONS, AND INDUSTRY PUBLICATIONS.

Quantity discounts are available on bulk purchases of this book for reselling, educational purposes, subscription incentives, gifts, sponsorship, or fundraising. Unique books or book excerpts can also be fashioned to suit special needs such as private labeling with your logo on the cover and a message from or a message printed on the second page of the book. For more information, please contact our Special Sales Department at Ultimate Publishing House. Orders for college textbook or course adoption use.

Please contact Ultimate Publishing House Tel: 647-883-1758

Wire Publishing is a registered trademark of the Ultimate Publishing House - Printed in the United States

Strong Mind, Lean Body by Tony Greco

ISBN 978-0-692-08247-8

TONY GRECO

STRONG MIND
LEAN BODY

Strategies
for Life
Success

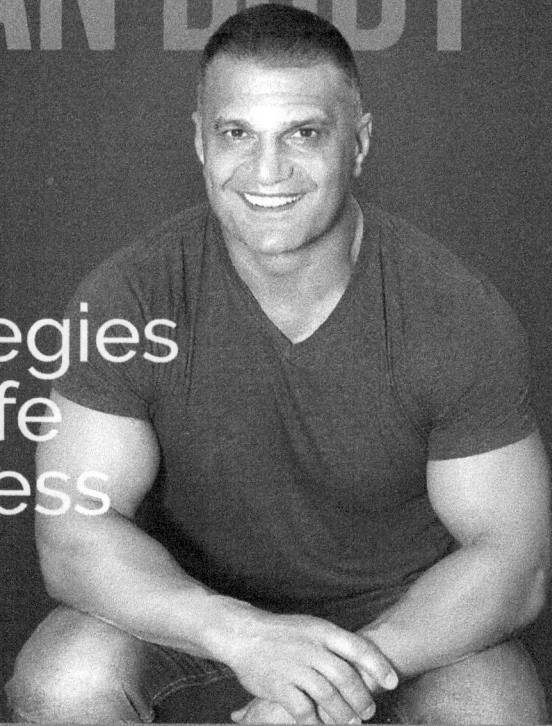

Foreword by Carol Alt, International Supermodel

DEDICATION

For my girls, Amelia and Ava

ACKNOWLEDGEMENTS

I f you're brave enough to dream it, it can happen. You have to be determined that no what it takes, you're not going to stop—not going to quit or give up—until your dream becomes a reality. I am here to help you make that dream a reality. It's in your heart, unleash the lion and defy the haters and pigeons and the people who say you can't. Ask yourself WHY you do the things you do every day. FOCUS on the WHY and focus on VISION—a clear vision and mind and lots of energy that will be contagious, that will bury the losers and haters and uplift the positive ones. If you're not the leader of the pack, the view never changes; it's yours to get. Make it happen!

So many people have helped me live this philosophy along the way. Here I acknowledge them because they have put up with a lot—and inspired so much in me.

I give gratitude and thanks to God, my savior.

To my wife Lisa, my best friend who uplifts me every day—thank you for your love, patience, and for allowing me to be able to wake up next to you every day! To my girls Ava and Amelia, who I love so much and hold in my heart every day. To my mother and father, who sacrificed and encouraged me to never quit or give up, and always to believe in myself that I could make things happen. To my sisters Wilma Milito and Lilla Sicoli who brought me up, watched over me, and taught me that families love, no matter what!

To my business partner Paolo Fiorin, who helped me go through obstacles and our cherished ups and downs, and who shared the same vision and helped me achieve the direction and path to success. To the Greco franchise, which has grown into something that I am genuinely proud to be associated with.

To my friends: Andrea Calabro and Tony D'angelo, who gave me strength, knowledge, and your time and expertise through tough times in my life, I will be forever grateful. To Johnny Giannetti (Preston Hardware) thank you for your encouragement and always reassuring me that I am making the right decision. To Scott Miller my lawyer and friend thank you for the advice and guidance and the legal support. To Romeo Agostini and Pompei Balestra, who are always there to lift me up and provide a good dose of humor. "What a life!"

To all my friends at La Bottega: Pat and Rocco Nicastro and Johnny Adamo. All of you have provided unconditional support throughout the years. To Nino Coco from Giovanni's restaurant, thank you for the amazing food and fabulous wine. You are the most unselfish person. I know you always say the right thing.

ACKNOWLEDGEMENTS

To my martial arts instructors John and Peter Douvris, Robert Loyer, Steve "Nasty" Anderson, John Savidis, Jim Flood, and Mike Bernardo, thanks for the inner strength—mind, body, and spirit.

To my workout Crüe: Chris Lacharity, Tony Maatouck, Joe Lolli, Gino Milito, Adam Fata, Ramsey Sayah, Pierre M.J. Poilivre, and Dr. Dan Seller—you guys are so uplifting. The laughs and choice of music for our workouts always has been, and will always remain, a classic. To my clients who constantly inspire me when I'm helping them, and therefore helping me to remember that all things are possible. It's teamwork! Thanks for sharing your private physical lives with me. I feel blessed and privileged to be your trainer and mentor, and a part of your path in life to help you live lean, live fit, and live well.

To my niece Rosa Sicoli and nephews Matt Sicoli and Franco Milito, I am so proud of you guys and for seeing how you overcame the obstacles. Your dads would be so proud of you, and I know they are looking down on you every day. To my cousins Vince and Roberto Borrelli, for always having my back, and to all my teachers and coaches who believed in me. To the Milito family: Gino (again), Val, Carlo, Piero, Tony, Frank, Art and Rachela, and Adriana. Special thanks to Gino and Val for being the BIG brothers I never had.

To Carol Alt, I am blessed to know you as an amazing mentor, a friend, model, actress, and to enjoy your wealth of knowledge in the health world—especially for your knowledge on raw food. I am grateful for you and the good things you always bring in this world, Carol.

To Steve Warne, my co-host for the Greco Lean and Fit Show. Thank you for being such a great collaborative partner. To the team at Bell Media CTV

TSN 1200 CFRA. Special thanks to Leanne Cusack, Liane Liang, and Kurt Stoodley. And to Steve Warne, my co-host for 11 years of Grecosize radio show on TSN 1200. Thanks for mentoring me and sharing your knowledge and friendship.

To all the professional athletes and celebrities whom I have had the pleasure to train and to learn from, showing me what it means to be normal and modest despite the fame. I thank you Carrie Underwood, Mike Fisher, Claude Giroux, Dan Boyle, Marty Havlat, Randy Robitaille, Todd White, Dan McGillis, Luke Richardson, Chris Phillips, Paul Byron, Brendan Bell, Fred Brathwaite, Tyler Toffoli, Jason Akeson, Marty St. Pierre, Darrel Powe, Peter Schaefer, Jason Bailey, Jody Shelly, Brandon Manning, Brad Rempel of High Valley Band, and Kevin Dillion. Brad and Curtis Rempel of high valley band

To Richard and Roberto Valente for feeding me while I had my jaw wired for a month. Rob, I know you continue to support me from up above.

To my childhood friends: Luigi Paravan, Joe Merlo, Guy Ouellte, Claudio Sicoli, Robert Strmota, Frank Decaria and Domenic Crupi, Robert Fata, Tony Lefebvre, and Gabe Antonini—so many memories. To my good friends Pierre Poilievre and his wife Anaida. Both of you always inspire me and make me think nothing is impossible. "Hey! You a nisa guy." To my good friends Matthew Perry (cover photographer), his amazing wife Angela Beauvais, and their beautiful daughters Nadya and Kylee. You all continue to support my dreams. To my good friend Charles Schachnow, whom I can count on and continues to provide unconditional support in everything I do. To my friends Todd and Janine Marcotte, thanks for teaching me "who you are, what you want."

ACKNOWLEDGEMENTS

To Bruce Engel (criminal lawyer), my wingman.

To Danny Seller (Dentist) thanks for keeping me smiling

And… to Felicia Pizzonia, who gives me strength, knowledge, and uplifting positive energy. You're unbelievably creative and talented as a publisher and coach, and an amazing friend. You are so positive every day, which helps me to see my vision better. You are a true gem! A big heartfelt thank you, to the Ultimate Publishing House team. The process was truly impressive and enjoyable, thank you!

Finally, to my parents Albino and Rosina Greco. Without your love and support, I would not be the man I am today.

And to all the great humans in the world! Thank you!

CONTENTS

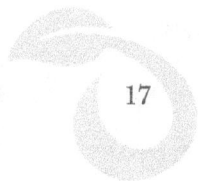

FOREWORD BY CAROL ALT

Regardless of who you are, what your past story is, or what your future holds, you likely desire to have a good, high quality life. How you go about achieving that in the way you envision it is where differences are made. It goes beyond hoping for it and requires action on your part. You have to consider the food choices you make, pay attention to your body and how it allows you (or hinders you) in doing what you love more optimally, and be mindful of your mental and emotional wellness. To me, fitness is what ties all these things together.

So many people feel that fitness is easier said than done, and yes, it does take work, but the work is a rewarding component in your life. *Strong Mind, Lean Body* is an instant "must have" resource because it offers a passionate and power-packed perspective on what it takes to start your journey to a stronger, healthier you. Tony Greco has hit the pulse of the important message about fitness by touching on all the areas of it that are essential to a high-quality life. On a personal level, I've spent time with Tony training and seeing his boundless energy and commitment to helping others become better—and it works!

What I find most refreshing about this book is that Tony gives us all the blessing to be who we are, and reminds us that we are beautiful as we are, that the human experience is about more than having a "perfect body." It's about having your best body possible. This includes a combination of mental, physical, and emotional balance. Combine that with better food choices and the realization that fitness is yours for the taking, and you'll know that you are the only one who can stop *you* from experiencing the best results you can. When this happens, your life gains meaning. Your U Seed© will grow and flourish, bringing out your vibrancy in ways you may not have previously realized were possible—before embracing the message and calls-to-action in *Strong Mind, Lean Body*.

Enjoy this book as I did, and don't hesitate to live fearlessly for being your best self possible.

Carol Alt

International Supermodel, Actress, Entrepreneur, Raw-Food Enthusiast, and Author

www.CarolAlt.com

SEEKING THE GOLD MEDAL

"The best way to predict the future
is to create it. Make it happen!"

TONY GRECO

Mark Twain stated that the two most important days in your life are the day you are born and the day you find out why. I admit; I can't remember when I was born, but I remember a huge day in my life vividly to this day.

I walked into my new preschool classroom one day and had zero idea of what I was going to say to my classmates, much less what to expect. Not because I was shy or fearful, but simply because I could not speak English. It was 1974 and my family had just arrived from the mountains of Southern Italy with $500 and a new rent payment of $465. Now we were in the substantially bigger Ottawa, Canada area. Back home we were known as "paisanos"—peasants—but my parents' hopes for us were to become more.

That day, despite not knowing the language, there was one belief that had already taken root inside me—I was at that place in time because I had an opportunity. My parents didn't speak English, either, but they were determined to give my siblings and me a better opportunity for our lives and didn't hesitate to sacrifice a great deal to do so. Then there were Dad's strong Italian father words in my mind: *you better not blow it, or else*!

These messages from my parents were powerful and occasionally stressful. Out of good-intentioned desires to motivate, I was reminded constantly that I had better do what it took to become a doctor or lawyer, or else I would be a loser. I knew two things. First, I didn't want to be a doctor or a lawyer. Second, I did not want to be a loser. I just had to focus on what I did want to be and create a plan.

The powerful lessons from my parents have played an intricate role in the person I have become. Because of it, I had an early on understanding that when you want something you either stand up and fight for it, or sit down and sink.

Being active and a love of sports were two outlets I had to help assimilate into my new world of opportunity. I was an energetic kid, focused on what I did and where it would get me. Don't confuse that with challenge free, because that wasn't the case. A particularly big challenge happened in sixth grade when I was going to get some Kentucky Fried Chicken for lunch, out of all things. A group of kids came up to me and the odds weren't good—like 15 to 1 not good—and they began to push me around. Their mission was to pummel me and I wanted to fight back. However, a previous message from my dad stopped me. "You ever get in a fight, Tony, and you'll really have a fight on your hands when you get home."

That day I stood there and took those punches. To my ribs, to my face, to every exposed part of my body that they managed to sneak a punch or kick in on. It hurt, and my pride hurt more. It was a horrible experience and when I got home and my dad asked what happened, I explained. From that day forward, I had the nod to fight back when necessary. That was the catalyst to my life as a rebel, a title I still proudly hold today.

What is a rebel? A rebel is someone who disrupts the expectations of others and understands the strategy and patience it takes to make the right moves in any situation.

Soon after that event I enrolled in martial arts. My dad didn't believe in spending money on things like that so I started to work a paper route to pay for it myself, and then added two more. Committing to the martial arts gave me a forum to learn how to fight and defend myself. Humbly today, I admit that at first I had the sole purpose of wanting to unleash the animal within me and hurt others if they tried to hurt me. I wasn't going to look for trouble, but if someone came to me looking for it, they were going to get the worst end of the deal. This is not a part of the teachings or beliefs of any sound martial arts program, but at that time it was who I was and how I felt—it was my will.

As my rebel was released a strange thing happened. This forum I had found for my aggression calmed me down. I began to develop discipline and better understand how I could use it for more than power in the traditional sense. I could use that discipline to empower myself, and others. Now the rebel had a cause. Everything came together in a way where I could:

- More clearly manage problems—which we all have at times;
- Ensure my efforts were focused on achieving goals that were meaningful to me;
- And, recognize that my output and mindset worked together to deliver the outcome.

This mentality is what I took with me in everything I did, and saving money became even more important, so in addition to the paper routes I started a job at the Ottawa International Airport. I began in the kitchen and was a dish pig—or more pleasantly sounding, dish washer. This job was tedious and boring work, which meant that I had to keep myself rooted in strong reminders of why spending that time was worth it for my goals.

My time at the airport became an intricate part of my growth and development. A desire I had was to save up for that car my parents would never be able to afford to buy me. Taking the bus to-and-from work was obviously fine for others, but I was not content with it. Then there was the work environment. I best compared it to what I imagined a prison kitchen might be like—both a literal and mental prison. There was poor ventilation, no windows, and little enthusiasm amongst my co-workers for life. I couldn't imagine feeling that way, day after day, year after year.

When you look at everything you have to do as a growth challenge you become better through your actions.

What I was doing for work was something considered menial to others, but because I understood that I did not want to be in that airport kitchen forever, I worked hard and set little goals for myself to make my days more interesting. The more I did this, the more I advanced up the kitchen ranks at the airport. Yes, they do exist. I went from dish washing to filling the small plastic bags that held utensils, salt, pepper, and sugar. If you've ever flown you still get those on your tray. I bet you never wondered how or where they were made. At that time, a great many of them from the Ottawa Airport were made by me. After proving myself there, I was good enough that I got promoted to sandwich maker.

I eventually graduated from high school, still no clue on what I was really going to become, and with another promotion to a different position at the airport—this time, outside the kitchen. I was out on the ramps with these guys, working with baggage and I thought it would be such a step forward for me. It became much more than that—it was a wake-up, make that shake-up, call to remember what I knew I *did* want and *did not* want. I was surrounded with people who had no vision for their lives that was greater than making it through that day. Really, they had no goals. This happens to people and it's neither good nor bad. They either just didn't know how to go about finding more or they had surrendered their "more" for some reason, likely long ago.

When you stall, you've got to tune yourself up and get going again.

While I was at work one day, I happened to mention that I was saving up for a car. But not just any car—a black Corvette. The guys thought I was crazy—a disillusioned kid—but to me, that car was symbolic of what was important to me at that time, from my young guy's perspective. It was a reminder that I was meant to go places in my life and that it would admittedly be a great car to pick up girls in. Plus, it was a really cool car. I was so vested in my vision that I could practically feel the rumble of the 5.7L V8 on my foot as I pressed the gas pedal down. It was powerful.

During this time, I was also working toward getting my Black Belt in my martial arts discipline, and the pace of my life was aggressive and really focused. I was hyper aware of how every moment mattered. And by 1992, this work paid off. Two significant things happened:

1. I earned my Black Belt.
2. I was able to buy my black Corvette, a car that is in my garage to this very day as a reminder of where I have been and where I still have to go.

Two big goals were recognized, and it was time for the next step; I just had to figure it out. This was when I really understood the value of focus and looked to martial arts and fighting more competitively on the circuit to see what opportunities may exist there.

I started competing on the North American circuit, where I was seeded fourth in my category. I lost a lot of fights during that time. My discipline was tested and my refusal to be a loser was revealed on a bigger, more physical level. I'll never forget my first fight. I was only going for thirty seconds when I got smacked in the nose. It was bleeding so hard and I was thinking, *blow it off, you've got this*. This self-talk was the difference between bowing down in defeat and walking away a winner that day. There was also a badly busted jaw incident in there that compelled everyone who cared about me at all to encourage me to quit. But I refused.

You have to believe that nothing is going to stop you. You don't just go halfway and not finish what you started.

I had understood discipline in the dojo, but realized it was also necessary in a fight, even an organized match. Without it, you could not win. Things became real in 1995 when I was fighting in the ISKA (International Sport Karate Association) and kept advancing to the championship round. That match was a fusion of my thoughts, energy, and training. After seventeen minutes of continuously going, even after a massive punch to the nose, I went toward opponent after opponent with one thought—that of a winner. All these guys from these countries across the world wanted to win, too, but I didn't want to leave a doubt in anyone's mind that I was the one who wanted it most. Finally, the last opponent was before me—a guy from Austria—and on that day, after fighting to victory, I received a gold medal.

There I was, a guy born in Italy and having to earn everything I had up to that point in life, winning a gold medal. It was a defining moment in my life.

Being a guy with a black corvette and a gold medal seemed cool to many at the time, including me. However, it was what those two things symbolized that became a driving force in developing the person I wanted to become after that, and this is the man my people most identify with today. Mark Twain's words of wisdom about discovering your "why" had finally been recognized.

INSPIRING OTHERS THROUGH OPPORTUNITY

A gold medal speaks for itself in many ways, as it shows that someone committed a lot of time to doing something they connect with as best they could. That's all well and good but it's the heart of the gold medal that means the most to me in my life. It's a sign of training for three years, and a mindset that with focus, perseverance, discipline, and the ability to follow your own command, you can do a great more than anyone might ever give you credit for.

They say that a gold medal winner gives 40% of their mind's effort, compared to the standard 5%. I don't know if that is true, but what I do know what also matters is the drive you have to begin—it can stem from pain or pleasure, so long as you know how to use it effectively. My drive to reach that point initially stemmed from pain; the pain of being bullied by a bunch of kids and of all the tough expectations my family placed on me. Some might have wilted, but today I am grateful to those experiences and two of the most incredible mentors I could have—my parents.

Tony Greco
I.A.K.S.A. World Champion

I now had stronger awareness of how attitude is everything and that nothing is impossible if you believe in it and want to do it. You can make it happen.

This was exciting and liberating. I'd found my way to do something big, something that mattered. I decided to achieve this next level of success by opening my own martial arts school.

Having this school connected me with the role of being a teacher and a coach—someone who didn't just show another person how to do a specific movement, but also how to develop a strong mind that would go with that physical awareness of what the body was capable of. A martial arts experience is only as good as the teacher allows it to be, guiding and nurturing students in both the physical and spiritual aspects of the sport.

An evolution began, one that took me from one Greco Martial Arts school to multiple. The need to reach out to more people who wanted and craved a good experience for their mind and body transitioned the martial arts component into Greco Lean and Fit, and then into Greco Fitness, until the chain of fourteen facilities was sold in 2017.

Knowing where I am today causes me to reflect on my life growing up—on my parents in particular. When I think about the way my parents managed their life's struggles, working at the jobs that were most available for people who didn't speak English, I am in awe of how big they did live—in mindset. They instilled urgency in me to succeed in my life and I don't take that for granted. In fact, I am so grateful for it. My parents are the type of people who could win the lottery today, but it would not change the way they live. The disciplines they have in their simplistic life are ones that many people discredited back then, but strive to achieve today.

- They ate organic foods from their garden. This was because they couldn't afford to buy it, but it gave them good fuel for what they faced.
- They didn't need to be friends with the world, but those who they were friends with meant something.
- They didn't add unnecessary stress into their lives, such as living outside their means. Because of this, they paid off the mortgage on their home in ten years.

What they had, I see many people seek today. If I can connect you to the philosophy, mind, and inspirations to make changes that make you better, you will find that you have built the heart of a gold medal winner. Period. This information is for everyone who wants to go beyond desiring changes in their life and on to achieving those changes. Whether you are a receptionist, mechanic, or celebrity, your struggles are the same. I've heard these things from people of all backgrounds and experiences.

Most people cannot connect the "say" and "do" together, and as a trainer there is only so far that I can push you. The rest is up to you. You need to have the mind to push yourself ahead and the body to give the output you require.

When you work toward these types of improvements you feel *so good* about yourself. Little advancements mean a lot and they keep you moving forward. I am not saying you have to be skinny to accomplish these goals, but when you feel good about yourself you do things a lot better compared to someone who doesn't feel that way. That's human nature.

If you have doubts or excuses, you need to toss them aside. I am a firm believer in keeping it real, and know that you can do this if you receive compassion when necessary and straight talk when needed.

Don't let anything hold you back.

You are meant to be in the body you were given, not someone else's body, even if you consider it ideal. Be who you are designed to be unapologetically. Have no doubts that you can do this if you set your mind to it and put your body into motion. You're not meant to be docile, regardless of what your life entails.

MY ASSURANCE TO YOU

This book is going to take you to that next step in developing a strong mind and lean body, regardless of where you are at this very moment. It's the start, and the destination is in your capable hands.

The mind is what gives your body the discipline it needs to make changes that impact you positively. Your body is meant to be in motion and carry you through the experiences that define your life.

This is what you can expect to happen as you touch on every area that will connect you to your inspired purpose:

1. **To recognize what your initial goals are**
   Perhaps you want to lose weight, regain flexibility, or feel more energized. Your "why" is important to understand.

2. **To recognize that you have negative self-talk that needs to stop**
   Your thoughts and comments, whether said lightheartedly or not, are the director of your experience. Poor thoughts cannot lead to a stronger mind, which means doing whatever you can to wipe out negative self-talk and replace it with positive self-talk is required.

3. **To recognize what your obstacles are**
   Believing that your preexisting circumstances stop you from gaining strength and accomplishing new things physically and emotionally is a thought barrier you must break. A busted-up knee doesn't mean you have to be unfit. A broken mind doesn't mean you should never try.

4. **To recognize what you truly want**
   When it comes to fitness pursuits, as you progress you often realize that there are underlying desires that are also important to you. Often times, you did not think they were important at first or you finally opened up to what will keep you excited about your "why" and the benefits of achieving it.

5. **To recognize your successes**
   Intention and action lead to success with everything in life. As you nurture your growth and treat yourself lovingly, you are going to come into your own and reach that point where you do think, *this new place I am at is even better than I'd envisioned it would be.*

Surrender and be heard. Read, absorb, take action, and repeat as often as necessary. I don't want to motivate you, as motivation is temporary. Make this book your resource and constant reminder to be inspired to explore and recognize your fullest, amazing potential. It's there. You have it. Your newfound knowledge is going to become your power, with you being the accelerator that puts it into action.

Inspiration is what sparks the change inside of you and resonates with your true self. Use your emotions to build your vision and go beyond hoping, to doing.

CHAPTER 1

THE U SEED©

"It's not about failure; it's about trying
something and risking something
for attaining your goal."

CAROL ALT

When I got my Black Belt in 1992, I thought I had a plan for everything. But as Mike Tyson said, "Everyone has a plan until they get punched in the face."

During a big fight in a tournament, I scored a point with a hit to a guy's ribs. The problem was that he was already in full motion with a spin hook kick that landed swiftly on the side of my jaw. Blood flew everywhere and I was completely dazed. The ref came over and said he thought I should be done, but I refused. The paramedic on site came over and tried to encourage me to stop and he finally convinced me.

Off to the hospital I went and there I waited, now in some very serious pain and still waiting for an X-ray. After the X-ray was completed many hours later it confirmed what I had suspected—I just had a bruised-up jaw. So I went home, but that night my face started to swell up so badly that by morning, I decided to go to my dentist. On the way to the dentist, I got a call from the hospital. They'd made a mistake and my lower jaw was fractured in two places. The excuse for missing it—a new radiologist. I returned there and was offered little more than some pain killers and the advice to take it easy.

Since I still had my dentist appointment I made my way to that appointment next. When he saw me, he immediately freaked out and sent me across town to a hospital to see a guy he knew that specialized in jaw injuries. Long story short—my jaw had to be wired shut (for 2 months) and it turned out that if I hadn't, I would have had to have it busted and realigned soon. I was in shock...and pain. So much pain.

Now when it comes to pain, I'm extremely stubborn. I don't like to take any medication, as I view my body as a temple. The staff at the hospital told me that I'd have to spend the weekend there and that they'd be giving me some morphine and other things for the pain. I refused and it threw them off, to the point of where they didn't really know what to do with me. And I was so glad I did, because I just sensed how it would mask the pain and not really help me live with it. What happened next was what I had believed would take place. By the next day, I felt great because I'd allowed my mind to remain thinking strongly and confidently that I could conquer the pain, more so than it would be allowed to conquer me.

I didn't do it just be a tough guy or to cling to my self-professed stubbornness. I did that because of something that existed inside of me that I'd worked hard to cultivate—my U Seed©.

Your U Seed is what controls your outcome in every situation.

THE 9 PARTS OF YOUR U SEED

There are 9 key parts to our lives that, when working together and being nurtured, give us the opportunity to grow into our destinies and recognize fulfillment on a high-performance level. They grow the roots that connect the body and mind together in way that allow them to best work together.

These are the 9 parts of the U Seed:

Health

Your health consists of what actions you take to ensure that both your body and mind are being nurtured to their fullest potential through your mindset, movements, and nutrition.

Self-Image

The way you think about yourself is the way the world will receive you. Your beliefs about yourself show through your actions more than your words. Creating a vibrant, positive sense of self-worth will help you grow into all you can be.

Love

Relationships are an intricate part of how your life's experiences define you. Recognizing the power that happens when you act and respond from a place of love will allow you to build up relationships that are good for you, and in which you are good for others. This includes both your personal and professional life, as well as even casual acquaintances.

Money & Career

You need money in order to provide for yourself and your family. Likewise, you most likely will receive that money through your career. For most people, large portions of their every week are devoted to working to make money, which means that you want to have a great relationship and attitude about both. Learning to embrace sound financial decisions and earn money from a career that will bring you gratification, if not appreciation, is important to your wellbeing.

Physical Environment

The physical environment you are in can either compel you to grow or drain energy from you. Just like a body is meant to move, the mind is most stimulated when it doesn't remain in one place too long. Don't limit your life to one small environment when there is an entire world of opportunity out there.

Vision

What do you see for your life when you think of your big picture, or even the small, joyful details? When we craft visions that help us move forward with our goals and pro-growth steps for our life, we are giving fuel that helps us take action. See it, believe it, and it can happen!

Mentality & Focus

All minds need to be stimulated in order to keep performing for us optimally. As you go through life, embrace every chance to learn new things and commit to the focus necessary to master that which makes you mentally and physically stronger.

Spirituality

The importance of connecting your heart and life's choices to a power greater than yourself is both liberating and necessary. You can control a great deal, but through realizing that there is something in this vast universe bigger than you, you can find comfort, strength, and resilience.

Play

Life can't be all work and no play. Truly. Having fun is the best way to receive the laughter that you need—Vitamin C for your psyche—as well as create special memories and moments with people important to you. It can even be you out on a solo recharging adventure. I can guarantee you, if you go out and have fun and movement simultaneously, you are going to have this crazy energy working in your favor a whole lot more.

What do you think about these 9 areas of your life? Are they excellent, average, somewhere in between? What's neglected? Visit www. strongmindleanbody.com and download the U Seed Growth Sheet and tap into your master gardener to begin to grow. Only you can do it! This book will help, as everything in it really revolves around how important the continual development of your U Seed is to all you choose to do—or not to do.

Everybody has a U Seed. If I were in a room right now with you I could point to each and every one of you and say, "You have it," repeatedly and I'd be right.

For me, my U Seed is what allows me to move through tough times, such as my broken jaw, and get back up and continue moving on.

When my jaw was healing I was committed to not losing a step and using that event as an excuse. Don't get me wrong, it was challenging, and even humorous a time or two. I went to the karate studio and was trying to teach, talking through my wired-shut mouth. I made it work, and my business partner still chuckles about my determination during that time to this day. Furthermore, I was not going to lose all this weight due to not taking in the proper nutrition so my mom—bless her heart—blended all my meals up so I could drink them through a straw and still get nutrition. During those two months, I only lost 5 pounds compared to 20-some pounds like many people do with their jaw wired shut. That was how I used my U Seed in that situation.

Take a moment to think about what life was like when you were first born...

As a baby, if you wanted food you screamed until you got it. When you didn't like it you spit it out. When you were unhappy, you cried your little lungs out until someone came and made it better. When you saw something interesting, you crawled to it. You knew what you wanted and how to get it.

Then came all the rules of life.

"Don't touch that." "Stay away from there." "Don't jump on the furniture." "Do your homework." "Be quiet." "Eat everything on your plate." "Don't hang out with that guy—he's bad news." "Go to university. Get a stable job. Get married." "Why don't you have kids yet? Clock's ticking."

Most of these are good guidelines and rules. But they teach us to do only what we think others want. And that is how a lot of people spend their whole lives—doing what others want them to. Is that you?

Are you unsatisfied with your bank account, your job, your body, or your relationship, but doing nothing to fix any of them? If you answered "yes" to any part of the question, your problem may be that you are failing to live up to your life's purpose.

Think of that purpose as a U Seed. Your U Seed is the reason you were planted on earth. For some, that seed never grows. It just stays buried. It sinks deeper and deeper into the soil until you cannot find it again, while other plants in your garden (some of them weeds) get all the sun, water, and the most fertile soil.

How are you today? How's your U Seed doing, and do you even know where it us? The most important element that everybody has is their U Seed. It's inside of you and you need it. If you are alive, life is going to bring you a series of planned and unplanned events. How you prepare for these situations will make a difference. This starts with your self-talk.

The person who hasn't nurtured their U Seed will say, "Oh my gosh, I can't do that." When you have nurtured your U Seed, you'll say, "So what if I haven't done that before, I'm going to do it now."

Life happens and it's tough, so no matter how you look at it you'll have obstacles, but they can turn into something positive if you have the right attitude. A U Seed *is* in *you*. I used it as a positive focus point in my life whenever I had bad karma and challenging moments. It was what uplifted me and helped to make me who I am today. This is how I know that when you face the obstacle of thinking you're going to fail, you can beat the obstacle by looking at it positively. You will grow mentally stronger, sometimes despite yourself.

What's your relationship with your U Seed? What are you going to do with it? You have two choices:

1. You can toss it into the garden and let it be smothered from light and growth by the weeds that take over.

    Or,

2. You can water it and nurture it so it blooms and rises to any occasion that you face.

The choice is yours; the outcome is of your own design.

The U Seed is in the middle of your heart. With your love and attention toward it, you will have the heart of a lion.

I had a hockey player I worked with once in a coaching and training role, and he was an only child player, great skater at a pro level. The coach called me up and said, "The kid is great, but he's got no frickin' heart." I knew the kid needed a spark that went beyond training. *He just isn't a fighter*, they had said. Maybe so, but that did not mean he didn't have the aspiration to become a better hockey player. The kid was just exhausted.

When a person is constantly bombarded with negativity it is tough to manage. This kid was no different. If he were to be graded, he was like an overall C that needed to be lifted to an A. How do you lift someone up to an A? For this kid, it was constant reinforcement to bring about a stronger mind to maximize his body. He had physical skills, but needed some emotional development. What I helped him do is actually the same as what you could do in your version of this situation. You need:

· Encouragement to step up and step out of your predefined beliefs of your limits
· To understand that conquering weaknesses equates to adrenaline

This book is designed to deliver both. Some of it you'll get right away, some of it will instantly feel familiar, and other bits will likely be so foreign that your first trained thought will be, *no way*. Remember, that is a thought of fear. You're moving past that.

IN SEARCH OF YOUR U SEED

If you entertained the notion that I'm lucky to have a U Seed, but you... not so much, think again. You just have to admit that you've lost it in that weedy, emotional garden, and start cleaning up so you can first, find it, and second, cultivate it.

Search your heart and soul until you find your U Seed. No one is born without it, although many struggle through life because they don't cultivate it. Don't accept that fate.

Be relentless in your pursuit of this. Breathe in and begin to search for what that certain quality or set of qualities is that gives you the resilience you need to keep moving forward in life, no matter what. These are your personal qualities that help define how you control your life and the actions you take. The place you can bring these wonderful attributes to light usually exists near the places where you feel and experience:

- Fear
- Insecurities
- Hesitation

These are powerful emotions that become stronger the more you enable them in your life. The first step to moving past them is to acknowledge them and then get to work on disabling them. They'll fight back so don't be blindsided by it, be prepared, because as quickly as those weeds grew over your U Seed, they can be cleared away in a single swipe. After that, it's just managing them and tending to your garden.

The beauty that takes place once you cultivate your U Seed is that it opens opportunities for other people to nurture and grow theirs—all inspired by you.

One of my most memorable U Seed stories comes from a client I had at one of my fitness centers. He came to a "day of reckoning" and reached the point that he had to do something to become a better person and role model within his family. It was a combination of feeling better emotionally and doing more physically—the epitome of the strong mind, lean body philosophy.

This client went more extreme than many people might consider necessary by putting a victory logo tattoo on his ankle. It was his constant reminder of "why" he was taking the actions he was; that no matter how tough a day may be, remaining committed and focused to the outcome was worth it. I'm sure his family fussed at first with some of it, because he made two significant changes right away:

1. He brought his entire family into the center to work out and grow healthier. The importance of him leading through letting them see they were all in it together was important.
2. He changed the family's entire approach to food. The fridge was filled with certain types of food for certain times of day.

This guy had a strong commitment and he surrounded himself with the right ways to nurture his mind and body at the same time. The results were exactly what he created them to be.

Through his actions, this client was also teaching and nourishing those people most important to him. This meant that through growing his U Seed, they were also watering theirs. This is literally a gift that will last a lifetime! That's the whole idea of this concept.

NATURE VERSUS NURTURE

When you are accomplished and focused on what you wish to achieve, others will take note. This can go one of two ways: it can be either good or bad. There will be some people who get it and are excited about what you are doing. They are not the concern you should have. Your concern should be those who aren't as excited about what you have achieved because it forces *them* to reflect inward. That can be painful, especially to someone who has no clue where their U Seed is residing.

AN IMPORTANT MESSAGE ABOUT FOOD

You know how easy it is to get distracted and not make the greatest choices for food in the home—taking convenience over quality. Kids are most always going to go right toward the unhealthiest thing you have, that food that is laden with corn syrup and artificial sugars, those ingredients that are highly addictive and dangerous enough they can lead to diseases that kill. By shopping healthy and paying attention to the outside aisles, which have fresh and organic foods, you can make the only choice a healthy choice. This way, no matter who resists at first, they will eventually clean up their mind and clean out their body by gravitating to the better choice. Human nature shows they will do this, and it is certainly preferable to starving.

When you get to a higher level of fitness, you're excited to be the first one to summit the peak and wave the victory flag. You've worked hard and earned it; it's a completely reasonable thought. If you went about this the right way you'll be excited to invite others up to the summit to stand with you. This is where the resistance often surfaces.

People are vulnerable to a natural high that occurs after you hold onto anger and anxiety for too long, often resulting in a vigorous desire to take people down...just because it will make them feel better for a short while.

Imagine two monkeys in a cage and in that cage is a ladder with a banana on top of it. Monkey #1 climbs the ladder to get the banana, only to be pulled down by Monkey #2. Monkey #2 didn't seem to care that it could have done the same thing, but it decided that it didn't want Monkey #1 to succeed. These monkeys represent human nature on our achievements. If you are not operating from a strong mental and physical space, you often intentionally or subconsciously wish others to fall to your level. The reason why you do this are revealing. It could mean:

- Envious thoughts
- A lack of confidence
- Laziness
- Feelings of being owed more than enabled

Humans are always trying to take other humans down because they haven't found their own level of fulfillment. You shouldn't give anyone that type of power over you and once you stop allowing it to happen, it's amazing how it can change into something positive and inspiring to your personal development and to others. One half of your battle is realizing that this will happen when you begin to transform and improve to meet your goals and the other half of the battle is creating a defense that doesn't allow someone else to jeopardize what you wish to achieve. And perhaps you've guessed it by now—that defense comes from united strength between your body and mind. When they work together, incredible things unfold.

One of the most important first steps that I do when I am teaching people is to educate them about the U Seed. This applies whether it's one-on-one coaching, a group session, or even a Skype session. I'm accessible to the world, because I know that there is a ripple of positive impact that can be had on a global basis, starting right from my home base in Ottawa.

Out of all the people and groups I have worked with, a story that really stands out to me about how something simple and easy for one person to do can truly impact an entire community exists. Through an initiative to send t-shirts, balls, shoes, some bikes, and other things to a group of children in an impoverished African community, they were given the opportunity to experience joy and inspiration—both priceless gifts. One day I got this video message from these kids, all smiling and waving at me. There were signs that read: *Thank you, Tony*. I watched it and was just amazed and my heart was a pile of happy mush. There was so much joy in all their eyes and they were in motion, so proud and excited and grateful. I know it meant a lot to them, but it was a reminder of why spreading good opportunities to people is so important in life. It was such an impactful moment. Every bit of work that it took to get that organized paid off a hundredfold. They grew their U Seed that day, and mine grew just a bit more, too.

Remember, don't make excuses, take action!

I know the stories of how people use their U Seed are far too rare, and I also know that there are many stories waiting to unfold—first to the person and then to the world around them. Maybe to you.

You may be nervous to start, but just keep in mind this wisdom: failing to plan is planning to fail. It's easy to get distracted with what you do not need if you fail to plan. These distracters stop momentum dead in its tracks and distract you to the point of where you forget what it was you wanted to do.

We can all do this. If you're a Millennial you fall into a stereotype of not having the skills to communicate and achieve what previous generations did. You do have the skills, they're just hidden. Start by looking at the world around you more than your phone, and determine who you are more than deciding who others *are* or *are not*.

The digital world is great but it's detrimental to people because they start lacking in focus, which means that their attention span is weakened.

There are those people who experienced life getting so busy that they don't take time for themselves. Please, grant yourself permission to pay attention to you. This is a time to be selfish, and it's for a good reason. If you are the person who does all you do for your kids, but has no energy for you, what good you are? You can root your growth in this source of pain. Or, if you think that you've got to do all you do because you'll paint a better environment for your friends and family, you can view your source of growth as pleasure. The choice is yours. Just grow. Make it happen by taking action.

MAKE IT HAPPEN!

I believe that if you want something the next logical step is to make it happen. Why would you intentionally not work toward something you wanted? It doesn't make sense. In order to grow your U Seed, here are three action steps you can take that will help you nurture your seed until it's strong and healthy.

1. **Answer the tough questions about U.**
    Who you are and what you want is important. What do you want to become? By deciding this, you are watering your U Seed and freeing it from the weeds and clutter in your emotional garden. Don't settle for less than being that beautiful flower that you want to bloom every year. For example, if you want to grow financially, find a way to understand your relationship with finances and make pro-growth choices to allow for that goal to happen.

2. **Manage your space.**
    You're going to encounter the unexpected every day, but you should not let those moments throw you off to the point where you don't stick to what you need to do for yourself. By training your body and mind to be on a high 24/7, you are instilling thoughts into your mind that make you able to blow off what isn't significant and work toward what truly matters. There is enough time in the day, contrary to popular opinion, but you just have to master it.

3. **Keep believing in the steps you take.**
    If you don't truly believe in something with genuine conviction from your heart, mind, and soul, you will struggle. By absorbing your belief into your every thought and action you are naturally growing your U Seed.

"Keep your dreams alive. Understand that to achieve anything requires faith and belief in yourself, vision, hard work, determination, and dedication. Remember all things are possible for those who believe."

———————

GAIL DEVERS

CHAPTER 2

U REST, U RUST

"It's never too late, or are you too far gone, to start exercising. If you don't, your body will not function the way it should and the quality of everything you do will decrease. It sounds harsh, but this is reality."

TONY GRECO

Not everyone is thrilled to hear this, but the reality is that if you rest, you rust. The body isn't meant to be dormant. It requires exercise to promote four important aspects of your well being:

1. Energy levels
2. Muscle strength
3. Maintaining a healthy weight
4. Improving your brain function

The older you get, the more you have to worry about all these things. Have you ever heard, "If you don't use it, you lose it?" It's true! With all four points listed above, this can happen... But it doesn't have to.

Why settle for stress, weakness, weight struggles, and a less-than-optimal brain if you don't have to? I have yet to meet a person that is not drawn to the benefits of the four items listed above, and exercise is the solution.

ADDRESSING ENERGY

Once upon a time in your life, as well as the lives of all your ancestors, a natural energy existed in the body that they could take for granted. There were things to get done and regardless of how long or taxing a day was, everything got done. Then, depending on the situation, you got up the next day to do those same things again. This constant movement proved itself to be good for the body.

My hometown of Calabria, in the province of Cosenza, is in the southern mountains of Italy, and for my parents it was a long walk down to the village. There were no cars and roads, either, because we were poor people in a poor community. I remember what my parents had to do on the weekends quite well during this time, although I was so young. They'd take an animal and make their way down the mountain and into the village about once a month, making a 30km trek, and then sell the animal, buy food, and make their way back up the mountain to our home. Sounds exhausting, doesn't it? Yet, my parents managed to have the energy for it each and every time. It was completely natural and they were prepared for it.

The same energy existed in my grandparents. They had moved to Canada for a bit in the early 1960s, but found that Italy was calling them back. Upon their return they built a home nestled in a mountain valley so they'd have land to farm. This was no easy feat and it required them to make 12 trips a day, totaling about 20km, to get the sand and stone to build their 2800 square foot home, which was called L'aria Rossa (Red Air). That land provided food for my family, and helped to feed families who didn't own land to grow food on. The number of lessons from this story that have flowed over into the way I strive to live my life is large, and I am so grateful to know these things.

For centuries, our bodies served a specific function that demanded it have energy. You had to seek shelter, hunt, and handle all the tasks that guaranteed your survival. No laziness was allowed, and being lazy could cost you. Today, we've grown lazier, and that is what has to change. Lazy people simply cannot be energized people. It doesn't work that way.

Over time, everything has become more convenient and now we don't have to do as many things for ourselves, and it has created changes in how the body reacts within its environment. So many people do not understand that.

Today, people often choose to wait for the closest parking space to the store they want to visit. I cannot imagine ever actually preferring that close spot over walking from the back of the parking lot. How about you?

You've got to earn your calories.

Take this lethargic scenario: you pull up to the convenience station and wait to park right by the door. Once you get that coveted spot, you go into the store and shuffle over to the soft drink machine and get the biggest size they have. You pay, walk your few steps back to your car, and start slurping on infinitely more calories than what you have even begun to wear off. Depending on your lifestyle, you may have just taken in nearly all the calories you should for a day—and it's all sugar.

People come to me and ask what I can do help them get more energy. That's one of the biggest concerns they have. The best way to demonstrate how they can achieve that is to go back to the car example, because people get that. In fact, people usually treat their cars better than their own bodies. Think of your heart as the engine of your car. Are you going to put sugar in the tank, or nutrients and good sources of food to keep you running efficiently—and in better condition to go the distance? You're probably saying "nutrients" for an answer, but would your actual habits say the same thing? Think about it.

The more energy you have, the more fun you will have in life.

If you walk down a flight of steps and feel winded it is going to impact every part of your day, from how you go about preparing for your day all the way through making it through.

Energy also has a link to your diet. If you put crappy food into your body you're going to get crappier results. You'll also be at risk of getting bad cholesterol (LDL—low density lipoprotein). High levels of this cholesterol are a big problem in today's world, and one that can be addressed *if* you are willing to do what it takes. I can't tell you how many times I've heard people say that they can't work out because they have high cholesterol. It drives me crazy, because, in fact, I've seen the results of what happens when you take people from high cholesterol problems, on medicine from their doctors, down to medicine free and healthier. So, to anyone who suggests that to me, I say: "Maybe, but if you follow what I teach you and give me three weeks, we can change that." I look at it this way:

- Who wants to be on a drug for the rest of their life?
- Who would choose to keep a serious health condition if they could get rid of it?
- Who embraces heart disease over experiencing life with people they love?

No one! That's who. Pills are not the answer, not only because of their side effects that put you at risk of even more serious stuff. Exercise is the answer, and it will give you a great deal of what you need in order to be energized and healthier.

When I'm in a room full of people and trying to emphasize this point I have no problems giving people the finger. Okay, I am simply pointing it toward them, but it gets their attention. I know it may be considered rude to some, but I am so passionate about wanting people to get healthy and I want them to know it. I cannot emphasize it enough.

THE IMPACT OF MUSCLE STRENGTH

We all have a skeletal system and what happens is that when you stay active you keep your muscles, joints, tendons, ligaments, and muscles flexible. If you're sitting in a chair you can just get up—when you're young. Other people, as they age, start ignoring the activities that give them muscle strength. Before you know it, they're dropping down into a chair and need to use their hands on the arm rests to help them get up. And it only gets worse. Suddenly they're shuffling, and then going to a cane and to walker, maybe even a wheelchair. Unless you have a specific condition wrong with you, the root cause of this digression is a lack of muscle strength.

Active people show that the aging process and a lack of muscle strength do not have to go hand-in-hand, at least not to a severe extent.

My dad is a great example of a man who hasn't allowed muscle weakness to impact his life. He can still garden all the time, getting up and down without any aches and pains, and it is still rewarding to him. The bonus is that he gets to continue to eat healthier because of the fresh vegetables he grows. That is the type of person you should want to age into. It is the best option, hands down, because most people are going to have to work really hard for most of their life. Then they retire, and what? Do you want to suddenly do nothing, or do you want to do and experience more?

One thing I get so jacked about is when I work with someone who is a bit older, maybe forty or fifty, and they want some help improving their muscle strength. They can sense it's changing and they've decided to defy it. They're committed to the process emotionally, which is actually about 70% of the battle. And the rest is a commitment to the exercises and movements that will strengthen the muscles and the core. Maybe you do squats, pushups, or some other body weight exercise. There are so many proven ways to improve muscle strength and most of them don't take a bunch of bulky equipment. They only require that *you* take the initiative to do it.

You can end up being stronger in your life at the age of 50 than you have ever been before. When you start improving every year and feel you're at your best self yet, you will be happier and more physically confident and assured. That look on someone's face when they realize this is awesome. I never get sick of seeing it, and will always enjoy when my clients share these successes with me.

MAINTAINING A HEALTHY WEIGHT

The illusion of a healthy weight can be very different from actually having a healthy weight. Human nature dictates that many people will judge someone by what they *are* or *are not* just by the way they look. If you go to the gym and see that chunkier aerobics instructor you probably think, *they don't look fit.* For them, they may have a healthy weight and it's completely different than what it may be for you. Imagine how silly you would look if you cut off our head in a picture and put it on the neck of a body that you perceive to be "ideal." It wouldn't look natural or right. A healthy weight makes you look natural and right with the body you've been given.

You do not have to be a calorie counter, but the more exercise you do, the more you have to eat. And the less you do, the less you need to eat.

The more muscle you develop, the stronger your metabolic rate is. You need more of the right foods in order to maintain a healthy weight and to burn fat, not muscle. The more muscle you have, the more calories you burn. You could see that skinny woman who looks great in a bikini, but gets winded walking up a flight of stairs. Is that what you really want? I hope not, because it's not healthier. A healthy weight is tied to muscle, not being able to see your ribs sticking out.

If you are someone who needs to lose some weight do so. You'll learn some great ways to manage that in the *ELMO: Eat Less More Often* chapter. By losing unhealthy weight you also:

- Look better
- Move better
- Boost your metabolism
- Increase your self-esteem

For example, a woman may come to me and say she needs to lose 20 pounds. All of a sudden, she has this number in her head, and she feels she'll be better if she just loses it. The problem is that number has nothing to do with what your body fat level is. That level could be excellent. At that point, it becomes a matter of toning and tightening to get that illusion you weigh less, when you possibly will not.

How you feel will always be more important than achieving a number that you created because you felt it was ideal.

If I were face-to-face with you today, at this moment, this is what I'd tell you: "Let's get you to a healthy weight. Forget about the bikini, because you're beautiful just the way you are."

STRONGER BRAIN FUNCTION

You've learned some amazing benefits of exercise, but the brain is the most important tool you have to use. Don't neglect it and always focus on nourishing it. The U Seed offers you a blue print to use for developing and maintaining stronger brain function. If you want to download a copy of it for your reference, please do so at www.strongmindleanbody.com.

Your brain, computer, data base, whatever word you want to use, is what guides you to whatever destination you wish to go. Ultimately, the main thing is that you have blood flow and these oxygen levels in your brain. You release these brain chemicals like serotonin and dopamine. They are all present in the cells of the hippocampus, which is the part of the brain—a part that basically serves as the main circuit board of your brain. Vigorous exercise is the one thing that has been noted that can improve the release of these good chemicals in the brain and work toward maintaining stronger brain function.

More so, for anyone who is stuck trying to solve a problem in their life, they have found that by exercising and releasing endorphins and those other happier chemicals that come from the brain into the system, they were able to simplify the problem enough to come up with a solution. The way I look at it: Who has the time to dwell on something for two hours if you can go have a great forty-five minute workout and walk away with the answers you need?

I'm just asking you to move.

By no means am I saying you have to go work your butt off and instantly transform into something that really doesn't work for you yet, because you are not there yet. If you do that, you'll be training your brain to

CASE STUDY

John J. Ratey, MD wrote an interesting book called *Spark: The Revolutionary New Science of Exercise and the Brain*. When I read this, it was fascinating, but one study that was shared particularly stood out to me. Brain cells shrink and then grow again when you exercise and all these studies were done with kids to do these tests on an annual basis. One of the test groups was in New Orleans, an area high in crime. One group of kids there were put through vigorous exercise for forty-five minutes a shot, five days a week. The results were incredible. Their academic grades went up and they showed a more positive outlook for their life. Now this is a fraction of the entire concept, but it highlights how much exercise does impact the brain.

work against you. You know those thoughts—oh, I'm so tired. I'm so sore. This is so hard. All negative stuff that you don't need. One of the hardest, but most necessary, things you can do is wipe out limiting self-talk because it will never inspire you to do the simple task of moving. Again, just move!

WHAT HAPPENS WHEN THIS ALL COMES TOGETHER?

My client Marilyn Wilson, owner of Marilyn Wilson DreamProperties/Christie's International Real Estate, is a busy and successful high-end Realtor in Ottawa, who has stamped her imprint on the multimillion-dollar home market. Her story is as inspiring and incredible as is her no-quit personality. She refuses to give up once she sets a goal for herself.

To give you an idea, Marilyn works hard and enjoys an exciting life, filled with the bells and whistles that success cultivates. This is all great, of course. But what does it mean without your best health possible? A place in time happened for Marilyn where she realized that what she had materially wasn't necessarily consistent with her physical well-being. Her time and career demands were just too hyper-focused on everything aside from her health.

When she first came to me for help, she neglected her overall well-being for some time, and she had a big event coming up—a class reunion. Because of the pace of her life and the lifestyle she'd transitioned into, she was carrying excess weight and was to the point where she would feel fatigued just going up and down a set of stairs.

She didn't know what to do, but I knew just how to start helping her.

We began to work together and developed a routine focusing on flexibility and stretching, for starters. She was committed to this, because as I said, she refuses to lose when she commits to a goal. After only three months, the results were noticeable. She could easily run up and down stairs without being winded, and she lost 20 pounds.

The lesson that Marilyn carries for everyone who truly seeks change is a powerful one. Despite her schedule, she never forgoes her weekly personal training sessions—and she trains like an athlete of 25! The benefits of this are immense. She is able to persevere throughout her day with unlimited energy, which means she can accomplish everything her schedule demands of her. Her daily workouts are a significant part of this strategy.

Everything has continued to grow in Marilyn's career and her personal happiness due to her efforts. There was no sacrifice, only the best kind of gain—that of self-improvement. If you were to ask Marilyn about this, she'd be the first to say she hasn't sacrificed one bit to achieve her fitness goals. Actually, her business increased after she began to pursue fitness because she had the energy to do what she needed to do, and do it better.

As a trainer, I see Marilyn's positive attitude and feel her contagious energy every time we talk or workout. It draws you in and I can see why people enjoy being around her energy and joy. It rubs off on you.

What do I want you to take away from Marilyn? The story is not limited to her—it can be yours too! It's about being committed. Using age and work schedules as an excuse doesn't cut it, not with me. Because I know that everyone has the time to do something, regardless of how busy they are. I can't make the days longer, but I can give you the energy to enjoy them more.

MAKE IT HAPPEN!

I want you to wake up tomorrow morning and know, without a doubt, that you are grateful to be alive. Not everyone will have that same opportunity. When you start your day, commit to making something new happen. Do these three things and you are giving yourself the opportunity to feel a lot better than you may have in a long time. It's the 1-2-3 power punch to make sure you don't grow rusty and you are choosing to be ready to go!

Move by:

1. **Breathing deeply—even before you get out of bed.**
   Breathe in deeply and hold it by your diaphragm. Feel how the oxygen fills your lungs and body and be aware of it. This is actually a form of meditation, another good practice to do daily. Then think about how grateful you are to be alive and have the opportunity to do something great with your day. Also note—a side benefit of deep breathing throughout your day is that it makes you aware of posture.

2. **Drink a lot of water.**
   Water is really important because hydration is necessary and as you get older, enough water helps you to eliminate aches, pains, etc. My personal goal is that if you aren't peeing clear every time you go to the bathroom, you're not drinking enough water. Pay attention to these simple things so you are equipping yourself to make it happen.

3. **Exercise in whatever way you can.**
   Depending on your fitness level, do something just to move and get started. If you sit at a desk all day, maybe you can stand up when you talk on the phone or just to stretch your muscles, or even walk around for five minutes every hour or so. You can also choose stairs over elevators; any decision that gets you moving more is a good start.

   If you have joints or areas that experience chronic pain, be gentle with them and do other things that will help you. You'll also be surprised how deep breathing exercises and drinking lots of water can assist with this. Everything works together.

"Stay true to yourself, yet always be open to learn. Work hard, and never give up on your dreams, even when nobody else believes they can come true but you. These are not clichés but real tools you need no matter what you do in life to stay focused on your path."

———————————

PHILLIP SWEET

CHAPTER 3

CUT THE NOISE

"There are always distractions,

if you allow them."

TONY LA RUSSA

S nap out of it! If you are tied to your smart phone, technology, and other gadgets, you are also missing out on other important areas in your life. One of the biggest risks you face is losing that strong mind that you came into this world with.

People get so wrapped up in staring at these small devices more than the world around them. The only other person they really take note of is themselves on the screen after they have taken another selfie.

Let me ask you: when you're focused on that small picture on that small screen, how can you be focused on the bigger picture of life?

If, at the end of the day, you're missing the big picture you are likely putting obstacles in your way that hinder you from any type of positive growth and true accomplishment. You're missing the mark when it comes to creating the experiences that will make your life a whole lot better, in all areas of your life.

A distracted, narrow focus will impact:

- Your health: posture, hormones, and even weight can suffer from focusing on the noise more than the mission.
- Your career: more often than not it's impossible to give a best effort when you're constantly distracted. The formula of looking at your email every five minutes doesn't lend to the type of focus and effort your work likely requires.
- Your relationships: if you spend more time on your phone than looking at the people you care about face-to-face, you are missing out on one of the things that makes life most special—the people in it.

If you want to have overall happiness in your life you've got to have experiences and then share them with others. You can tell who doesn't do this, because they are often the same people you took note of on their way up, but they are suddenly on their way back down. Just be grateful that you have a chance to do things to keep you growing and moving upward. Make sure to never lose the accessibility to yourself so you maintain your ability to learn.

UNDERSTAND HOW YOU LEARN

We all have different ways that we learn best. Some people are aural, which means they like sound and music. Others are linguistic, preferring to use words in both their speech and writing. Then you have those who are physical and they will go off of movement, using their body, hands, and sense of touch. And then there are those who are visual, which means they like pictures, images, and spatial understanding. One of these four methods is likely to be dominant for you and you may have some others that work effectively in conjunction. You've got to know what's best for you. As an adult, you can take control of this. This is harder for kids to do because of the standard requirements that most classrooms have for them all—and that is where they spend a lot of their time.

This is what I know about me: I could read twenty textbooks and probably absorb 10% of the information, if even. This doesn't make me a bad person, but it does demonstrate that I have to rely on other means to really make the most out of what I learn. And learning is a requirement—just going on a computer to look something up isn't a substitution for learning.

The only high-tech computer you need to invest in is one you already own—your brain.

Again, cut the noise!

When I'm doing a seminar, I see people avoiding learning all the time, whether it's intentional or not. They'll stare down at their phones and they overreact. They read a text and respond, and I can see that they didn't even take the time to read the text thoughtfully because they're already in response mode. You know how I know they're distracted? They don't even realize that I see them.

Yes, we've all been guilty of this type of distraction at one point or another. However, life's biggest events don't happen through the phone, they happen through engaging with others and learning lessons along the way. You should demand to learn in two ways:

- By taking in what interests you so you can grow as a person;
- And, by being aware of the constant learning lessons that take place around you.

Honestly, these electronic distractions make me sick. I have two kids and it takes constant positive reinforcement to look beyond the electronics and to everything else. It's tough, but necessary. You've got to instill this awareness in your kids that life is not meant to be like that. Just because your friends have unlimited access to technology doesn't mean that you're going to do the same thing, especially knowing how it can end up impeding your growth as a person, and your brain health too.

You have so much information to use for great things, so stop being absorbed by the light and tap into your brain.

Think about this… Was any world problem ever solved through texting and selfies? No, it was solved through focus and ingenuity. This is where your talents will come out and you can learn to be a difference maker, not a blinded follower.

DEVELOP YOUR TALENTS AND IMPROVE YOUR SKILLS

Everyone has talent, but far too few people develop theirs. Days are so busy and in all the decisions we make in our six second attention span and those 50,000 plus thoughts a day, we seldom focus on talent development. This shows how lost in thought we can be and therefore clueless about pursuing what may be ideal for us. To stop this, it's important to take the time to connect with your "self," as that is when everything worth having begins to grow and develop.

When you're connected with your "self" you are also in the moment and it's amazing how much you are able to see and do. I think far too many good people overreact and think about the past, instead of focusing on the present. Sometimes you've got to cut the noise and take your lessons from the past, and then look to the present and the future. These are moments in time that you can create.

Train your brain so that it becomes a habit to avoid distractions and focus on how you can grow and develop your skills and passions.

Over the years I have come to realize that one of the best techniques to cut the noise is to learn to become a better listener. When you are listening in the right way, you are in the present and paying attention to what is happening with the person you're listening to (or even the group of people). You can get so much out of listening to someone and by giving the brain a rest from those exhausting distractions. Instead, you're fueling the brain with good energy that helps to develop your talents.

Few things are more frustrating than speaking with someone who you suspect didn't catch a word of the conversation. These are the moments when chaos can erupt between peers, friends, parents and children, and even with complete strangers. No one likes to say something to another person and think they weren't even worth listening to. Cut the noise and allow yourself to be present in everything you do. If you want/need time to dedicate to reflecting, do so, but not at the peril of everything else happening around you.

By taking the time to become self-aware and quiet those distractions that tempt you, you are taking the time to find and nurture your U Seed.

No matter how long you've lived in distraction, in this moment you have the opportunity to be born again, to start on a new path. Your skills and talents will only develop to their greatest potential when you allow yourself to be able to give them the proper focus. Always get better—that should be your goal.

ACCESSING YOUR SUBCONSCIOUS MIND

If you think your life is a mystery, you probably haven't sought out a trip to your subconscious mind in a while. We could never be "all knowing," of course, but we can know a lot about ourselves through the silence and clarity that exists within the subconscious mind. This isn't guru stuff, it's growth stuff.

Sometime back, I took classes so I could receive my yoga certification. The reason I wanted this was because of my martial arts background and the focus on mind, body, and spirit that comes with that discipline.

At the end of each class we would do a meditation. This was so we could get to know a state of relaxation. A small passage would always be read at this time and I felt how it helped remind me of the importance of that release for the mind—as well as the body. My favorite passages focused on remembering to "chill." At times, you can hold so much tension that your mind, body, and muscles don't relax. And they need to.

When you carry tension with you throughout the day it drains you on every level, making it impossible to do anything you have as efficiently as you could be doing it. This is when you have to stop and breathe in and realize that you're not in control the way you need to be.

You have to feed the subconscious mind calmness and be present in order for it to begin relaxing and pull you into the present moment.

Feelings of relaxation coming over you are so liberating. You can immediately notice the difference and identify with how good that place is. This is why it's important to calm yourself through breathing, meditation, or whatever you choose daily—so you train your subconscious mind, just like you would a muscle, to know what's best for you. How you train your mind means everything in correlation to the results you get. There is no other pathway to cut the noise than going through the mind. It takes time to master, and just like you can't do one bicep curl and have a big bicep as a result, you can't have a mind that can bring you to the present if you don't work your mind to try and master it. You need repetition.

I've found that visualizations are a powerful way to help achieve this. When you picture something in your mind, you start to slow down on everything else and simply focus on what you are seeing. If you place yourself living in the moment, no confusion and chaos around you, you will develop a stronger mind and a clearer vision for everything you want to do, including a commitment to fitness.

Guided meditations are also effective ways to learn to tap into your subconscious mind. During a guided meditation, someone is talking and taking you on a journey that incorporates your senses and draws you in. It's a good and soothing journey, one to make you feel confident and assured of good outcomes and what your thoughts are in this good place of achievement.

In my classes, guided meditations take place with people lying on their backs, their eyes closed, and facing upward toward the ceiling. At that point, the meditation begins and you start guiding people to that place you want them to reach. To give you an idea, this is one of the meditations that my clients really like:

Pretend you're in an elevator and you're going to the fifth floor. You know that five people are going into the elevator and three people are getting out. Good, now take a deep breath. We're going down to the fourth level, and now...

Then it's the third level, second level, and then first level. With each level, you focus on something that makes you become more relaxed, moving from head to toe until your body is completely relaxed. There's no tension—just you feeling this light shining right down from the top of your head throughout the body.

With a guided meditation you get into a state of relaxation—the quiet mind—and when you do, it's amazing how much you can absorb.

But until then, you've got to cut the noise. By doing this you will discover:

- Actions, words, thoughts, and ideas you may have otherwise missed
- A way to connect to yourself that has eluded you
- Less tension
- More direction on what you have the potential to do

The process of peeling away the layers to get to what's at the surface may take longer for some than others. It depends on your levels of tension and how much you really struggle to cut the noise. If you cannot cut the noise it's like having a small, weak muscle. In order to strengthen and develop it, you have to begin training and be committed to the actions that will help build strength. Only you know how much tension you are feeling and how long you should consider effective techniques like guided meditations to calm you down. It may only take ten minutes, or it could take up to a half hour. Regardless, it is time well invested in learning how to reveal your talents and tap into your subconscious mind.

MAKE IT HAPPEN!

The habits that have led you to this moment are not going to disappear simply because you want them to. You have to will them to change and take meaningful action to make it happen. By putting forth a committed effort to shift to new habits that promote self-awareness and a strong sense of presence in your subconscious mind, you will learn how to cut down the noise more easily and naturally. Everything will be positively impacted because of it. Remember:

1. **Take the time to prioritize.**

   I'd love to say, "Hey, ditch the cell phone and all will be taken care of," but that isn't how it works. By prioritizing things on a scale of 1-10 and not giving all your attention to low priority tasks, you will find less noise and more productivity for what is most important.

2. **Commit to focus.**

   You see a shiny object and you need it. That's a thought many people have, but this is not true. It's a false pitch that distracts you and really indicates a lack of being present. By taking a pause and thinking about why something is important or necessary, you can become a more focused person.

3. **Take massive action.**

   You can't just say what you want and expect it will automatically happen. It requires massive action, which means that you have to crank it up. Don't say you want six-pack-abs and only do ten crunches a day and think it'll happen. It requires doing more—maybe three hundred crunches. And it doesn't stop there. You also have to look at how you're fueling your body. How far will you go? Your answer should be, "as far as it takes."

"Massive action means being willing to make whatever shifts are necessary in order to achieve what you say you want."

———————

TONY GRECO

CHAPTER 4

FITNESS IS THE NEW MEDICINE

> "The body is a temple. We're meant to move, and this is why exercise is the new medicine. It helps us heal, just as much as it works toward prevention of many diseases."

TONY GRECO

More drugs, medications, and "cure-all solutions" are on the market than we can count. They market promises and hopes in big, bold letters, and put the side effects and disclaimers in small print that is barely noticeable, or in a person's voice that's talking faster than an auctioneer so you don't really hear the less appealing side of that drug or product. Is that really what you think your only option is? Yes, some people need to take medication for something, but more often than not, they are buying into a psychological concept more than a real solution.

Fitness *is* the new medicine because it offers a solution to all those people who take a statin drug just to feel better. They take something that has a placebo effect, but forget to consider the consequences of all those other chemicals that are going into the body—and your body is a temple. Take antibiotics for example; they are easily prescribed for colds, infections, etc. but when you take them, you need to counter their impact with a probiotic which mitigates their negative effect on the body. Do you do that?

This is why exercise is so important. It heals the thoughts of the body. Change and becoming better does not happen in a day, though. It takes time and commitment to become better. You go through changes, phases, and new moments of awareness, both physically and emotionally. And that is how you grow and identify why fitness is your new medicine.

THE 4-WEEK PROCESS

Most of my coaching and training clients make the transition to learning what their true intentions are for wanting to embrace fitness over a period of weeks. They don't know at first, even if they believe they do. It isn't that they were dishonest; rather that time revealed more of their story. This is where four weeks comes in, as this is often how long it takes for the real desires to reveal themselves.

Week 1
___

If you were to come into my club the first thing we would do is discuss goal setting so we could come up with a direction that would serve as a plan to guide us to the destination you have in mind. Maybe it's to lose 10 or 20 pounds. Having a goal as a starting point is important, enough so that I don't even work with a person who is not willing to go through this process.

Desiring change and not having a goal to assist in the transformation usually fails. With goals, you have a much stronger chance of succeeding.

During this first week you'll have lots of adrenaline and maybe a few nerves, typically, but you are already feeling better because you are actually doing something.

Week 2

During the second week, as a coach I often become the psychiatrist because people begin to open up and share their problems and how they've tried to solve them—sometimes successfully and other times not. "I used to have headaches, but I don't have them anymore because…" "I used to have confrontations with my husband (or wife) and now I have to do this…" Then they'll go on to explain that they have even divided out their fridges for their foods to get better, as they are dealing with a resistant spouse who still wants to eat everything that my client is trying to avoid.

There is always going to be a clash of opinion and fact when you start to change, which can be a challenge when it comes to those you love who do not want to participate in the change.

When you don't have support, you are vulnerable to giving up. Who wants another battle in their life, after all? And because of that, it becomes a defining moment. I can tell you, that if you stick with it, you'll end up grateful for your commitment. There are always going to be temptations around, whether it's via a person, food, etc. By having a goal and a plan and a support network such as a coach or teacher, you gain a plan for working through it.

Weeks 3 and 4

These two weeks often become those where, as a trainer, I become the marriage counselor. Now there are problems because of those clashes of opinions. Their spouses/others think they are doing this or that...they don't care what the partner thinks.

Fitness makes you find yourself mentally, physically, and spiritually.

This is why I believe it's a new medicine. Unless—God forbid—you have something extreme happen—like an accident—where you need certain medications and procedures done to help you recover, you should always remember: your body is a temple. And like I said earlier, it's meant to move and you can do so much better with the stronger mind, body, spirit connection you create through fitness.

All in all, even in as few as four weeks, you are suddenly thinking differently about the choices you are making. You can change your mindset, and therefore change your life for the better. "You know what? I'm not going to swallow another killer acetaminophen, because I can do things to avoid needing that." These small changes lead to bigger things and you start dealing with all situations in your life a lot better. You no longer need the quick fix.

MOVING FROM "THE QUICK FIX" TO THE FITNESS MINDSET

The cycle of fitness is centered on the time when you connect your mind, body, and spirit together. You do things in a way that treats your body like a temple, and your thoughts become more attuned to what is a good choice, compared to what is not.

You can't do this without being consciously aware of your choices, which comes easier through cutting the noise and focusing on fitness as the new medicine. There are a few things that you can do to start healing your body, which will absolutely make the rest of you feel better too. I recommend:

- **Swimming:** we all have this tension from our various demons or obstacles that only we can gauge. By swimming in the water a person will feel a lot lighter and good about themselves, even if they think they're overweight. There is less pressure on the joints and the heart muscles are being worked, which creates circulation to make your blood flow throughout the body. Aside from releasing tension, swimming helps eliminate inflammation, builds muscle strength, reduces headaches, and offers the benefit of movement.

- **Walking:** this is a great, low impact way to move the body and slowly build up endurance, either to run or be able to make additions to your walking that gives you a bit more cardio. It is also a great time to become more aware of the body because it is going to make you feel better. You'll start to see solutions just from this activity alone.

- **Running:** running is an excellent form of cardio and often one of the best releases a person can have to clear their thoughts and feel good. This vigorous exercise often results in what people call a "runner's high." A runner will get into this zone and get their heart rate up to 75% of its maximum rate. Everything is clicking and you feel great, not just because you physically ran, but because of the positive emotions it brings with it.

I know that not everybody is a runner or has a desire to be, but a powerful thing happens to people who commit to running. Take someone who runs a marathon or race, for example. They use their runner's high to cross the finish line. Maybe they have some aches and pains, maybe not, but to get to that point in their training, they've started to develop a new thought process. Instead of thinking they need a pain reliever for those aches and pains, they know it's going to be okay. The food they eat and their thoughts are going to help them heal. They're thinking, *you've got this*. That's the point when you begin to heal naturally, as opposed to with pills and placebos.

Your thoughts on what you are feeling matter because they begin the process of healing. Otherwise, you are masking a symptom instead of solving a problem.

When you move during exercise you put varying degrees of strain on your muscles. You push them to the limit and if you think of your muscles as a cable or elastic band, you can visualize them being stretched to their limit. That's what a workout really does. However, when the workout is complete and it's time to heal, via your brain you'll begin the process because you know what is supposed to happen and when. You exercise, you heal, you grow stronger, and you start again. Your body knows the routine.

When people stop exercising, things slowly begin to happen to their body. They may get back problems, for example. They go to their doctor and the doctor asked what has changed in their life. They say that they've stopped exercising. Aha! Now this person has muscles that are tightened up and that are no longer used to that process of healing. Of course, something's going to happen when you let the well-oiled machine that's your body turn stagnant.

The human body can endure a lot, which says something about its resilience when you consider how many people do not treat their body well. They live on a diet of sandwiches and soft drinks, and maybe have a vegetable about once a month. It's estimated that about 90% of people do not eat the right foods. That includes both those who think they are eating properly and those who admit that they don't focus on a healthy diet.

Your body is the ultimate healing machine. Through the course of exercise it gets to experience healing because of the good stress you're putting on it and into your mind and soul.

Exercise is a constant medicine, as it heals every single organ in your body that needs to be healed.

FITNESS AND MEDICINE FREE

High blood pressure and Diabetes 2 medications are highly prescribed. Yet, they are the ones that can most easily be eliminated from a person's life with a little initiative on their part.

I have challenged many clients to make changes in their diet and exercise to stop them from having to take drugs to manage diseases such as Type 2 Diabetes and high blood pressure. For the ones who accept, they most always learn a lot.

Before we begin, I have them go to the doctor to get their blood work done and levels tested. This way we know their exact ACL number or blood pressure level before we begin to work toward lowering those numbers.

I put them on a moderate routine of exercise and make some adjustments to their meal plan (more green vegetables and high-fiber foods). With their commitment, when they get retested three weeks later, many of them are able to say goodbye to the medications and hello to a new, healthier, medication-free solution. Everything becomes better.

Of course, not everyone is a three-week solution. For others, it takes longer for various reasons. Perhaps they:

- Struggle to change their lifestyle
- Have a more extreme condition
- Are not mentally ready to commit to the required actions

In these cases, I ask them to write me a day's worth of what they are eating and doing so I can review a more complete picture. My football coach used to tell me that a short pencil is better than a long memory, because I used to think I knew it all. So, write it down. That's the only way to see what's really happening throughout your day.

I think it's also a good idea to take a picture of yourself, because you see it and have to see it every day. This offers a constant reminder of who you are and what your story is. You can even take a selfie and look at it regularly. Remind yourself that you only have so much time. Ask yourself these questions:

- Why?
- Why Not?
- WhyNot Me?
- Why Not now?

There will never be a better time than the present to start making changes that you know you need.

FITNESS FOODS

There are certain foods that have properties that are good for you, all around. Making sure they are a part of your diet and come from natural sources is the key. You want to invest in the right foods. For example: canned spinach will never beat fresh spinach. The goal is to get the food you consume to be as close to the source of where it came from as possible.

Lean Sources of Protein

These include:

- Turkey breast
- Chicken breast
- White fish (from the wild)
- Omega 3, 6, and 9
- Walnuts
- Beans and Lentils
- Low-fat or non-fat dairy
- Tofu and other soy foods
- Pork Loin
- Eggs

These foods are filled with good proteins and good fats, which make them ideal for meals and snacking.

Low-glycemic Fruits

These include:

- Prunes
- Plums
- Pears
- Apples
- Berries (blueberries, Strawberries and Blackberries)

These foods do not interfere with insulin, the hormone that is associated with diabetes.

Vitamin C-rich Green Vegetables

These include:

- Broccoli
- Kale
- Brussels sprouts
- Spinach

Proper Supplements

Not all supplements are created equal, but there are certain times when a high-grade supplement is the ideal way to make sure you're getting the proper balance of the fitness foods you need. For me personally, I have such an active life that I need to have supplements to make sure I am getting the proper amounts of some nutrients. Protein is one example, because people who exercise a lot can easily be deficient of it, even with a good diet. My solution to this has been to create the Extreme Isolate 97 protein supplements because I control the quality of the product and I have very high standards and expectations. I won't take protein that comes from animals that have been fed antibiotics, which means that all my protein powders come from New Zealand, because I know they meet these standards.

The reason I do all of this is because both myself and my clients are busy. People who are on the go risk neglecting their diet. If you can have a protein shake to satisfy your hunger, give you good nutrients, and it leads to better performance throughout your day, why not do it? It helps.

When it comes to greens, nutrient rich greens come from more places than the garden. They also come from the ocean. Supplements such as Kurabie, which is also in my line, are effective because they have a very specific health factor. They take the best rich greens and combine them into one great combination that helps you detoxify your system and increase your energy.

TIP

If you are seeking out high quality supplements you need to look to a good vendor for purchasing them. Aaron LaBarre, owner of Popeye's Supplements, has a great reputation across North America and I know that he has the same discerning eye that I do for good supplements.

TOUGH, BUT LOVING CHANGE

I've never built my business on wanting money, because the mark of excellence comes from how people transform. Because of this, I will not work with people who don't want to go through all the steps to commit to a lifestyle, not just a program. If they just want an exercise routine, I'm not the guy for them, and neither is my staff.

One of the more memorable clients I had in the past was a lovely lady with a severe weight problem that was costing her greatly, both physically and emotionally. She would eat a carton of chocolate ice cream almost every night. Now that is pretty serious.

Her ex-husband was horrible to her and she was beautiful, but so sad. She'd already tried a doctor and a psychologist, but neither helped. Coming to me was her third, and perhaps last, attempt at trying to get out of the cycle she was in. She knew she didn't want to be there, but she didn't know how to escape.

She cried as she revealed all this to me and I felt such empathy for her, but I knew she needed something shocking. I told her, "You know what, when you go and eat that tub of ice cream tonight do it standing in front of the mirror and look at yourself. Think about it...you're adding more to your body. That's what you're doing to yourself." These were harsh words, but they worked. She finally got it.

This was the start of a journey and a transformation in her that is still going on today. And if you saw this woman today you would not recognize her as the same person she was. She worked hard and learned that fitness was her medicine. It wasn't the wrong foods or battling low feelings of self-worth—the desire to be fit cured those things. And today, she is at a healthy weight that is ideal for her. And all it took to start the process was just looking at herself in the mirror—really looking.

Let's face it, people look at themselves in the mirror all the time and they critique harshly. Guys look at their midsection and suck in their gut. Women evaluate everything, and this creates an impact and a mindset. You can either cower away from what you see or realize that you're also looking at the person who can start to change what you don't care for.

Only you can make a decision to change.

If you don't see yourself changing, you won't. However, when you start to visualize what a changed you looks and feels like, you are already taking action through a positive mindset to show that you do want to be that person that is more fit—and that definitely does not rely on medication to manage what you can manage on your own.

MAKE IT HAPPEN!

If you do not take any other medications, you are a rare exception in this world, and good for you. For those of you who take medicines, whether prescribed or over-the-counter, you need to get excited about the new medicine and start adopting the philosophies that go along with it. Try these three things:

1. **Take your first step.**
   If you do not exercise now, start doing something. Begin with a walk if you don't feel you can do anything more and build up from there. Find a coach, commit to a plan and a goal, and just get started.

2. **Get a picture of you naked.**
    You may have just gulped, and that's okay. You have to do this though, because the picture will not lie. It will tell you what you see at that moment and allow you to progress from there. By focusing on a picture over an actual weight, you can also more easily monitor where positive changes with your body take place, or where you may have to try a different approach.

3. **Give yourself at least three weeks.**
    It takes a certain mindset to wait for results to happen when you're impatient and eager to see them. Remember, you didn't get to where you are in just a day or two—not even three weeks—so don't expect that changing back will happen quickly.

"It's a crazy jungle out there, and if you don't take the time to do things for yourself, there will be a price to pay."

———————

TONY GRECO

CHAPTER 5

WHO U ARE, WHAT U WANT

"If you're not living what you love, you are just existing. Live the life of your dreams."

FELICIA PIZZONIA

STRONG MIND LEAN BODY

When you woke up this morning did you understand your purpose? So many people don't know what their purpose is. I could ask them who are you, what's your purpose, and why do you wake up the morning, and they would only be able to answer with an "I don't know" or "what do you mean?"

If you don't know who you are, you don't know what difference you can make in this world and in your life.

It's important to know what it is that you are doing, the reason why, and what impact that has on your life. You have to step back from your everyday rut and decide what you want, what truly makes you happy. You can only do this by sorting through all the parts of your life and seeing them for what they are. As you do this, all those weeds that are blocking out the good stuff in your life can be pulled, leaving you with healthy, fertile soil to grow your U Seed.

4 AREAS THAT DEFINE YOUR LIFE

FINANCIAL CONSIDERATIONS	YOUR JOB
THE INFLUENCE OF RELATIONSHIPS	OBSERVATIONS AND ACTIONS BASED ON YOUR HEALTH

When you look at the sum of your day, you will find four main areas impact most of how your day plays out. You will face:

- Financial considerations
- Your job
- The influence of relationships
- Observations and actions based on your health

Through understanding these four things, you can better understand who you are and what you want.

Knowing that money isn't everything, but financial security is

Financial security is not a set number, but a number that works for helping you live the life that you are designed to live. It's a different number for everyone. Do you need a thousand? Ten thousand? A million? You need to figure this out, because the amount of financial security you expect determines most of the things you do.

We all have necessities to pay; like taxes, food, housing, and all those other expenses that are a part of life. Knowing this can put a lot of stress on the body, and when you add in the stress of worrying about money, it impacts:

- Your relationships
- Your experiences
- Your opportunities
- Your health
- Your happiness

This is why finances are important. You have to know your number. If I spun a magic wand as you read this chapter and asked you what that magic number is for financial security, you'd probably stall because you don't know.

Most people have an equation that they have to work to make money and that is all that's involved in financial security.

Let's say you were a new person from a new country and you didn't have a dime and you were poor. I take you on an airplane and drop you off in the Big Apple without any money. The first thing you would likely do is seek out a newspaper and look for an ad to find a job. Probably at a restaurant, as it's the easiest job to find for the most part. You go there and tell the owner, "Hey, I'm from Italy. I don't speak English well, but I need a job." They'll likely hire you at a low rate and let you work in the kitchen as a dishwasher because in that role it doesn't matter that you really don't speak English.

Now you have a job and next you have to find:

- Food;
- And shelter,

And manage to:

- Pay for other basic living expenses,
- And find a way to save.

All these things take a little bit more of your money, but it's not really going to take you too far if you're not careful. If you want to move to a better situation, you'll either have to find a new job or start saving. This is where you can begin, even at a base level, to develop financial security. Even saving $50 a week makes a huge difference. The problem is, most people are not willing to make the sacrifices they need to secure the future.

When you are willing to sacrifice a bit in your daily life to build financial security you are going to benefit.

By learning your number and living within what it takes to achieve it, you are less likely to lose sight of it and what you must do to make it a priority. Additionally, this number is what gives you a realistic timeline. If you tell me that your number is ten million dollars and you're fifty years old, and you have yet to start developing financial security, what are your odds of success? Not great.

You have to find a number that fits your real-time situation. Maybe it will all change for the better at some point, and that's great, but you can only control what you know to be your situation today.

Developing stronger relationships

Whether you're married or in a relationship you have to determine if you're really committed. If you were to judge it on a scale of 1-10, with 1 being the worst, what would you score your relationship? This is important.

Do you like the person you're with? Are you happy? These questions need to be answered, and they should not be hard to answer, either.

Good relationships do not just happen. They have to be grown and nurtured over time, and with commitment.

If you're not happy in your most intimate relationships then you have some work to do so you can grow happier instead of continuing to grow apart. To do that, it requires new and different actions. Perhaps you commit to spending more time together, learn to communicate better, or even think about your sex life in new terms.

Gaining a better perspective on your job

You're not required to do what you love to do for a job, but trust me, it helps. I love what I get up to do every single day and that gives me a natural source of energy, in and of itself.

What happens when you wake up on a work day? Are you the "Oh yeah, I can't wait to get up and make a difference today!" person or the "Not another day, where's my snooze button?" How you feel at this moment impacts your entire day, and if you're not happy or content, you'd better look at the reasons why you're so accepting of that, and seek out something that will help you gain the right perspective on your day. Maybe it's getting up earlier to exercise first, or even meditate. These are two excellent ways to start a day with the right attitude—an attitude that indicates that you do know who you are and what you want.

A bad attitude is an indicator that you're miserable and something is wrong, not that there is something wrong with other people.

People who make differences and positively impact our world are more connected to it. For most of us, it feels good to do something that's good for others and ourselves, especially if we can earn a living doing it. Everyone has the potential to draw great things from their job, no matter what it is. For me, an important reminder of how the work I do impacts others came in 2012, when I received the Queen Elizabeth II Diamond Jubilee Medal in honor of my contributions to helping people. That felt great, and it was another reminder of why I love my work so much. When you have this type of connection to your work, even the most challenging day and/or situation is preferred to being somewhere else.

Taking notice of your health

It's very rare that somebody doesn't realize that there is something wrong with their health. All it takes is stepping on a scale or looking in the mirror to see that you need to lose twenty, thirty, fifty, or more pounds. When you clean your house and are winded after just vacuuming you can tell that you're not as healthy as you should or could be. The signs are everywhere, and you're a walking time bomb for even more trouble. So, what are you going to do about it?

As soon as you ignite that path to health and wellness, whether you're walking, jogging, sprinting, swimming, circuit training, etc., you will change all other thoughts in your life because you will feel better about yourself.

We all deserve to feel good about ourselves, and need to realize that only we can make the change. It's our job, not the world's to make sure it happens.

YOUR FIRST THOUGHT IS YOUR STARTING POINT

What is it that you want? If you don't know, start with the very first thought you have after thinking about it. So, if you thought "health," focus on that first. If you think of it as a 2 on that scale of 1-10, work to get it to an 8. Then move on to what comes next. If you think "relationships," and you

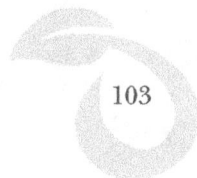

assess yours at a 3, make sure you work to increase it to a 9. Then keep going from there. Every time you see something that needs shifting, give it a value and keep moving to improve it. By doing this, you don't get overwhelmed and you still get results.

You have to ask yourself what you want to have happen with anything you wish to improve upon.

Through this process of growing into who you want to be and learning what you want you will find your purpose and you will be happy while you're doing it. If you refuse to change, you are also refusing to find your purpose. That's a pretty simple reality for a topic that likely seems complex.

Truthfully, 95% of the people in this world are not going to commit to doing the changes that I talk about here. It just won't happen, and that's okay. It leaves more room for people like you and me to strive for consistency in what we're doing. It's not about being perfect, it's about being committed to what you know you can control.

If you refuse to live your dream, you will only be a part someone else's dream who chose to live theirs. Is that what you want?

In my example, coming from Italy I recalled how it was expected to become a doctor or lawyer. I better do this or that or my parents will freak out. My coach said I have to do this or else… it goes on and on. We look to these leaders and mentors and all the pressure they put on us, often not knowing how to take it the right way. Their hope was to be a positive influence and their intentions were likely good, but guess what? By following their idea of our best situation, we lose ourselves along the way.

When we try to impress others we lose our true selves. Then we look at what we are not (or have not lived up to in others eyes) and don't even feel like trying. We didn't do what our mentors, leaders, and parents wanted us to do, so we start to think that we're garbage. We ask "why try" because we don't think anything positive can come from it. Before long, we're on the bottom of a heap of garbage and not even certain we can find a way out.

Many people live other peoples' lives and dreams more than is realized. You can tell this easily in today's younger generation. Go to a university and ask someone what they're studying. Maybe they'll say, "To become a lawyer." Then ask them "why" and they'll say, "Because my mom wants me to be." It's so sad.

Don't let this happen to you, because it is not necessary.

GROWING INTO YOUR BEST SELF

Many of my female clients happen to be ones that are overcoming something such as excessive weight and they are ready to shed what they don't need to start living the life they want. It's always inspiring and amazing. What is surprising for many people is the resistance that comes from those closest to them during this process.

Not everybody wants you to be your best self, so you have to be strong in your commitment to fulfill your purpose and do what makes you happy.

One of my clients was rather young—23—when I began working with her, and she had a boyfriend who was absolutely fit. They were the type of couple that most people naturally wonder how they ever got together, as they seemed so different.

When she came for help we discussed what could be done to shed some pounds and start to exercise more. We met weekly for a bit and then it moved to every few weeks after that and she was moving along great. Every time I saw her I knew she was following the plan. It showed.

With her new body came a desire for an updated image—which is a completely normal and natural desire. She began to buy really cool outfits and these purses that went with them. She looked like a model and she was being noticed by both women and men because of this positive energy she carried. Her problem was that there was one person who wasn't happy for her—her boyfriend. He got very jealous and it created problems in their relationship. They already had a child and were set to be married, but that plan had to go on hold. He actually mentioned that he'd prefer her to stay overweight—just to save on his own hidden insecurity (which he did not confess).

What would you do in a situation like this? It's not an easy call, and most people see the outcome as one of three ways:

1. Leave him
2. Stay with him and go back to the way you were
3. Hope he finally accepts the healthier you

Those are tough choices, but when you consider what life is meant to be, having health is one of the key aspects of it that can make everything else better. This is a lot to think about, and I saw what a challenge this was for my client. Marriage over staying healthy? No one should have to make such a choice, but many people are forced to. I can tell you this: I still hear from her once in a while and she's still committed to fitness.

MAKE IT HAPPEN!

Look, it all comes down to making better choices. You cannot know who you are or what you want if you don't commit to what you are doing and decide what helps and what hinders. This is how you start:

1. **Select your first thought on what you'd like to change.**
   Think of your health, relationships, finances, and career. Then take that thought and come up with steps you can take to start changing that picture. Just imagine...if you only have a hundred dollars in your savings account how much better you'd feel with a thousand dollars in it. Small and manageable steps are the key to big results.

2. **Visualize your outcomes.**
   For every change you want to make, put yourself in a place where you've already succeeded in your thoughts, words, and actions. Help to cement this in by thinking about this when you are exercising. It will bring everything together and you'll be working toward good changes that become healthy life habits.

3. **Identify with your true self.**
   Just going with the flow and doing things to appease other people takes you away from the direction you are meant to grow in. If you have challenges with doing this, you may have to start small. I'd recommend using the U Seed worksheet as your guide and motivator. It is built on your personal desires and inspirations, making it ideal for you to begin identifying with your true self.

"The best way to be successful
is to be fearless."

———————

JANELLE OSIDO

CHAPTER 6

WANTING TO WIN IS...

"You've got to have courage to win the game when there are so many obstacles in the way."

TONY GRECO

Without courage, your response to any situation in your life is sporadic, at best. There is so much negativity around and I have found that I must use that to make me stronger. If someone tells me I can't climb that mountain, I'm not only going to climb it, but I'm going to make it to the summit and look at the world around me.

There are times when you have to do something just to prove you can, and there's nothing wrong with that. It feels good and it reminds you that you can be limitless when you set your mind to doing something. If you say you can't, you can't, and if you say you can, you can. Period.

From my life's experiences, I have always had to be that person that needed to prove what I could do to others. It was never assumed, and I didn't have time to waste thinking it was unfair. I had to focus on what I could do.

Having to prove myself to others—and to myself—is something I thrive on. My gold medal is one of the best examples of that. People questioned every aspect of what I did during that time. The whole time I just thought, *wait and see*. It is okay to use others' negativity for your own good. Don't let anyone tell you differently. Build on that attitude that lets you know that you are your only obstacle to winning.

Wanting to win is...

NEVER ABANDONING AN IDEA PREMATURELY

Back in 1994 I wanted to put out a VHS tape called *Karatecize: The Tony Greco Way*. It was a VHS tape and this was way before Tai Bo came out.

I went to speak with a marketer who told me the numbers for it were off and I should not do it. It was a prime example of someone trying to dissuade you just because it didn't add up to them. In theory, I had no reason not to trust this marketing company, as they were very well respected.

I had the self-confidence, belief, and a vision that it would work despite what others said.

On the cover of the VHS was me with my black belt and a tank top on, along with my sixteen-year-old niece. I just sensed that it would be of interest, so what I ended up doing was going to all the Block Busters, and one of them was in my mall where I had my martial arts school at the time. I went in and talked with them and came to an agreement where I'd put the tape in their store for them to either rent out or offer for purchase to their clients for $19.95. They agreed.

We ended up selling 2,000 VHS tapes and that resulted in having the capital for my new location, which we called Karatecize. It was all cardio kickboxing and so popular with women back then. It was huge and that lead to starting the Lean and Fit Center and eventually fourteen locations in total. It all stemmed from this VHS tape and my commitment to win that fight.

You have to go with your gut belief to get you through the gate.

There's this old saying: real courage is knowing that you're getting lit before you start, but you start anyways. Listen to yourself and become aware of what you really want, what you're thinking, and how you act toward it. You have to keep a positive state at all times, even if you want something that nobody else believes you can have or win. This is tough to do, but once you accomplish it, it becomes a habit. Plus, what others say against you just bounces off. You just have to take the time to do it and get into that winning mindset. You cannot doubt that you've got this.

Wanting to win is…

TAKING ACTION TO BE MENTALLY STRONG

Today, there are about 200,000 people on their last breath. If you are not one of them you have a tremendous opportunity today. You can choose to:

- Laugh
- Take actions to be proud of your life
- Move
- Show appreciation for what you can do
- Follow your instincts

All these things keep the brain in a positive mindset, which means you'll have less risk of being:

- Negative
- Quick to anger
- Unmotivated

The more "on" you are, the more you can manage anything that comes your way. You always believe that what you are facing is something you can manage, no matter what it is. It could be a big decision, like promoting an idea you have that you believe is a winner, or even something small, like believing that if you commit to meditating five minutes on gratitude every morning you'll have a better perspective for your entire day.

Don't chase what you want, elevate your game and what you want will chase you" My good friend and client Claude Giroux proved just that by finishing the 2018 NHL season with 102 points, a hat trick which helped the Philadelphia flyers clinch their playoff spot of which I was there to witness, truly a historical moment.

TAKE THIS CHALLENGE:

Choose your favorite number and write the things that you are grateful for. If your favorite number is 9 (like mine is), you'd write down 9 things you are grateful for every single day. By doing this for three weeks, it's going to start becoming second nature to you and your mind will already begin to think with more optimism, gratitude, and a winning attitude.

When you follow this up with exercise of any sort, whether it's yoga, martial arts, or some other discipline, you put the physical and mental connection together. That is a sweet spot to be in, because everything starts to click. Your mind and body are working together and helping your soul at the same time.

I credit the martial arts for where I am today because it did teach me discipline and confidence. It became so much more than my initial intention, which was to learn how to beat people up.

It all comes down to what you are willing to do in order to create the life you would like to have. Look in the mirror and assess your efforts. Literally, take a few minutes to do this. I ask people to do this all the time and it's always an interesting experience.

A lot of people are funny, because when I tell them to do something like this, they are thinking, *you're weird*. Honestly, it's not me that's weird; it's those who are afraid to look at themselves in a mirror. The discomfort people feel by doing this often stems from them being lost in their own thoughts and feeling stuck in this game of life. They feel that they have to do certain things for certain results, but they don't act on belief for what they are doing—only what others say they should do. They blindly accept advice from a person or culture that doesn't know their private thoughts. By looking in the mirror, you can:

- Smile;
- Talk positively,
- And even laugh.

Doing all these things, even if it feels unnatural at first, will make you feel better. And that's where the transformation begins. Your brain starts to receive messages that you feel good and guess what, it starts to act in a way that correlates with feeling good.

The process of exercising the mind with positive input does make you feel better.

My emotions, my actions, and the way I feel do matter. And they do impact me.

Even breathing exercises are helpful for this. Next time you are doing anything and notice negative thoughts seeping in, stop immediately. Stand up and step away from wherever you are at and take 10 deep breaths in from the diaphragm. Focus on the air going in and going out of your body and connect your breath to your life. Think thoughts like, *I don't care what happens. This will be fine. I've got this.* Anything like that—just make sure that your thoughts are inspiring to you and how you choose to think and feel. And it may seem harsh, but at times, it is okay to not care what others think and freely think that. It's another way of using negative situations (or thoughts) for a positive purpose.

> "You can't just sit there and wait for people to give you that golden dream. You've got to get out there and make it happen for yourself."

DIANA ROSS

At the end of the day, you are the only one that can use "I" in a sentence. It's up to you to decide how you use it in your life. Nobody else will make anything happen for you, because they're only worried about their own lives.

Wanting to win is...

TAKING CHARGE OF YOUR OWN COURSE

I had a guest on my fitness show who had an inspiring story. This young woman had been told by her doctors that she would never walk again. She had MS, and they said it was going to be impossible.

Well, she didn't want to settle for impossible, she wanted to win.

This woman began to show commitment like most people can only imagine, or admire from afar. She began focused exercises that would build her strength and practiced walking, doing anything she needed to do to ensure she could walk. She would not take "no" for an answer. And over time, she succeeded.

After others had told her she couldn't walk again, she:

• Competed in a Spartan race
• Began a family
• Walked onto my fitness show

This woman's mental strength and physical determination made all the difference in her results. Stories like this always inspire us. Why? Because we all would like to think we had that type of determination and grit when push came to shove.

Every client who comes in to see me has a problem, maybe not as severe as not being able to walk or having a disease, but they do have some problem they want to address. It's most always weight.

The first rule of thumb for my facilities is that you cannot enroll unless you subscribe to the lifestyle.

The one-on-one initial consultation is a part of this process. The reason is that everybody thinks they know it all, but they do not. You have to go step-by-step. I start with measuring their body fat and going from there to see how much weight they have to lose if that's what they are hoping to do. They may be thinking "twenty," when in reality it's only "ten."

Necessary changes also extend to the diet. Of course, I am not going to be in a client's home to make sure they eat what I suggest, but I will tell them exactly what portions to eat in order to achieve the results they want. And if they stick to it, weight loss will happen.

What is often most interesting about addressing the diet is that I am telling people to eat more. They are like, "I'm here to lose weight and you're telling me to eat more." Yes, I am. People do not understand the impact of what they choose to eat.

It's not how much you eat, it's what you eat.

Think about animals. They have maybe 3-5% body fat and they are grazing all day long. Humans can be this same way. You have to accept that the food you eat creates the fuel you need for your day—regardless of where it takes you. If you were a car and wanted to travel from Ottawa to Florida you know it would take twenty-four hours. You realize that you'd have to stop and fuel up your car five or six times along the way. The same is true when you view your body as that vehicle that gets you to your destination. You cannot expect to get there if you let it run on empty. Finding a way to ensure it happens is how you take charge of your own course. No one can make you pull over and refuel—you have to take that initiative on your own. My good friend and client, Claude Giroux, captain of the Philadelphia Flyers in the National Hockey League, is a prime example of a person who wants to win, and he does win, consistently!

MAKE IT HAPPEN!

When you want to win, a natural result is that you take action. If you say you want to win and nothing follows, well, you're not being honest with yourself. Keep this in mind as you evaluate anything you want to do, and be open to attempting what you desire. This is the only way you'll develop the belief that you will win at anything you believe in and take action on.

1. **Write down twenty things you want to win at.**

   This is always an interesting exercise. Most often, people put the easy things down first or the more superficial things. I want a better car, a new wardrobe, etc. However, when it gets tougher to get to those twenty things it is the things that come up last that usually matter most. Family, for example.

2. **Develop a stronger "I" through your U Seed.**

   Take that look in the mirror and do what it takes to amp you up to realize that you are the one who is going to ultimately make every change you wish to experience. Get yourself excited to make it happen!

3. **Pursue an idea that you're interested in.**

   Whether you have an ambitious idea like what I had with the Karatecize DVD or a desire to take an art class (even if you can barely draw a stick figure), give it a try. It doesn't matter what others say, only what you decide to do.

CHAPTER 7

IGNITE YOUR BRAIN

"Exercise is as effective as certain medications for treating anxiety and depression."

JOHN J. RATEY, MD

Spark: The Revolutionary New Science of Exercise and the Brain

If you're not doing any kind of exercise you are missing out on your optimal intelligence. Physical movement, combined with the food that you choose to eat, does impact your brain function. When your brain isn't firing on all cylinders it's like a car that's spark plugs are clogged. It just isn't going to run as smoothly as it should. Why spurt and sputter when you can have a smooth ride?

One of the best resources I've come across to understand this whole concept in depth is that of John J. Ratey, MD, and the book I referenced earlier—*Spark: The Revolutionary New Science of Exercise and the Brain.* That book just blew my mind, and while I don't know Dr. Ratey, it's a book that I recommend to all of you if you want to learn more about the science of it all. For me, I want this chapter to give you the basics, because they do matter and I know that with them, you can make a significant difference.

So much is tied to exercise and being fit. Honestly, you may feel great and even look great, so you may not think you could be better. But by making sure you are always igniting your brain to operate at its fullest potential, you can find that all you do and touch upon has better results.

BETTER MANAGEMENT OF DEPRESSION AND ANXIETY

People suffering from depression and anxiety may not feel the motivation to go out and exercise. They'd rather do nothing, but finding a way to get some movement in your day can make a significant difference. There are both psychological and physical benefits to that movement.

By first considering exercise to treat depression and anxiety you could give yourself the opportunity to avoid taking medications for those conditions.

Physical activity is linked to:

- Easing symptoms of depression or anxiety
- Making you feel better
- Keeping concerns or previous conditions at bay, longer

When you release those feel-good chemicals, such as endorphins, you experience more calmness and a greater sense of well-being in your life. Those feelings are effective, and that peace-of-mind that someone who suffers from depression or anxiety can get must be priceless. According to many of my clients, it is the most relief they've felt in a long time. And suddenly they are craving something better for themselves, while also gaining:

- Confidence
- The ability to socially interact better
- A more "worry free" mind

By getting out and doing something you enjoy doing, whether it's walking, running, playing tennis, swimming, racquetball, gardening, or whatever, you are going to feel better. Suddenly you're thinking that you should have done that a long time ago. It always seems simple in hindsight, and that is perhaps the biggest struggle that someone fighting against depression or anxiety has to deal with.

CONCENTRATION

When you are exercising in a way that isn't just repetitive to the point where you "zone out," you have great potential to exercise your brain through having to concentrate on what you are doing. This could happen by:

- You doing something unusual in your movements that make you pay attention in a different way;
- And/or, you trying something new that forces you to engage the brain in order to perform the task.

Some of the exercises I do with my students force them to do something different. I may tell them they have to bounce a tennis ball off a wall and then every time they bounce it they do a squat. Some may be able to do it right away and others not. But the action requires them to think and focus. If they just held the tennis ball in their hand without the bounce, they wouldn't have to engage their brain in what they were doing.

You're encouraging your neurons to really work with one another and to create new ones that aid in thought processes and brain function. This is called neurogenesis, and it offers exciting promise for all of us, whether we're aging or facing challenges with our thought processes. When I first heard about this I was blown away. It's amazing. When you're doing that activity, you are more ready to ignite your brain than you would be otherwise.

LEARNING

I was teaching martial arts and there was a kid who was on Ritalin—a drug I didn't even know what was at the time. His parents told me he had ADD (Attention Deficit Disorder), and that's why he took it. Always wanting to understand things better, I began to ask a doctor buddy of mine about it. What he told me was intense. It sounded crazy, actually. He mentioned that drugs like Ritalin are basically a downer for a kid. It stops them from wanting to play and have fun and move around. It controls how hyper they are.

As a martial artist and someone who wants kids to be engaged in the arts because of their mental, physical, and spiritual benefits, I just couldn't get why that would be the first choice for managing a high energy kid.

Through the martial arts, I was able to connect with these kids who had these "diagnosed" problems and help them become engaged, have fun, and learn something new. I never saw the same challenges that the parents – and maybe teachers – had in a given day. It was a different approach, and a powerful one. This is one of the reasons that martial arts has become a solution for many kids who suffer from ADD, ADHD, and all these other conditions. Now exercise is viewed as a great solution to calm these kids down and as a result, help them learn.

One of the first things we teach kids in the martial arts is *pe wasa*, Japanese for hand techniques. There are twenty-seven hand techniques and you have to focus to get them done. Therefore, it has a positive effect on the brain as you try to learn these movements. The result is you gain intuitiveness and reduce distractions.

Sometimes the fastest way to calm a kid down—any person, really—to just allow them to burn the energy that has them distracted.

The topic of fitness being the new medicine has an entire chapter in this book, as you've already read, and even in children, the same principles basically apply.

What we do know is this: kids are not the only ones who have a hard time focusing on learning, which means many of these concepts apply to adults who take martial arts, as well. At the heart of it, when you choose to play, burn energy, and learn new things all at the same time, you are going to grow more confident in learning new things that keep your brain active and alert.

TIP

When you view fitness as fun and do fun things while doing it, you are going to enjoy what's happening for you. One of my most innovative business partner's, Peter Moore, is brilliant and known for HALO— Health, Active Lifestyle & Outdoors. Stimulating your brain while doing something outside—in nature—that is fun will ignite your brain. Playgrounds are not just for kids anymore!

PEAK PERFORMANCE

Whether you're an athlete or a business person, you need to rely on exercise in order to experience peak performance in whatever you do. It's not just the body moving, but the thoughts you have. You need to think and act quickly to respond to situations that happen—all at a moment's notice.

Peak performance in anything can only be achieved through being aware of:

- Your brain's ability to ignite
- Your body's fuel
- Your body's movement
- Your mindset and commitment

When you are striving to be a peak performer you are going to be aware of how everything you do—from thought to action to what you eat—impacts your goals and results.

Peak performers are a rare and impressive group.

What I really love about peak performers is that anyone can become one if they commit to it. Age, experience, and athleticism don't matter as much as your commitment. An eighty-year-old man can be a peak performer by training to run a marathon. A twenty-five-year-old woman can become a peak performer by committing to what it takes to become a CEO of a corporation by the time she's thirty. This is all possible when your brain is ignited and you realize that the formula for your success is a combination of thoughts, actions, and a continual quest to learn and grow. You live an ignited life, which allows you to sleep soundly so you can get up and do it all over again.

THE IMPACT OF ENERGY LEVELS ON THE BRAIN

I used to run a ten-week program for clients. To get them started, we'd do the typical goals that laid out an approach to diet and exercise. Then they'd come to meet with me on the third week to evaluate how everything was coming along. What people noticed during this time really goes to show what happens when you gain energy to do more.

Most people were just as excited about having more energy and focus as they were about reaching their other goals.

Suddenly these experiences were taking place that brought so much joy. Through their movement they were playing with their kids more, doing various tasks more often and better, and they began to associate movement with happiness and being better. They knew they were using their brain more and it felt great! And they wanted that to continue. This is the start of the motivation that can help you determine just about everything that's been covered in this book. It's incredible and those success stories never get old.

MAKE IT HAPPEN!

We all need a brain to live. By recognizing that it plays the most important role in every outcome we have in life, we need to be very alert to everything we think and do so we know that we're training it like it's a future Olympian. You cannot say you want to have a strong mind and lean body without striving to ignite your brain as much as possible. There simply is no other way to make it happen.

How do you start? Start by:

1. **Stop telling yourself you can't.**
    Negative self-talk is a toxic poison in your mind and you should know that anything you set your mind to is something you can accomplish. You may not get there right away, but so long as you

keep taking steps forward you have something to feel good about. Just keep moving up.

2. **Get rid of the excuse of time.**
   There is no more frustrating thing than hearing people use time as an excuse to not achieve what they want. Don't be one of those people. I get it, you're busy. Hey, I'm busy too. You've got to get your priorities together and decide what has to give, if something does. I guarantee that a lot of adults today could find an hour to exercise every single day if they decided to taper back on their social media or watching a television show every night. You do have the time, but do you have the desire?

3. **Acknowledge, Accept, and Adjust (3 A's)**
   Acknowledge that you have 168 hours each week. Accept that this is the time you have to craft a plan and act upon it for what you want. Adjust your current habits by taking your first step to start doing what will ignite your brain.

"Any man could, if he were so inclined, be the sculptor of his own brain."

_____

SANTIAGO RAMÓN Y CAJAL

CHAPTER 8

ELMO: EAT LESS MORE OFTEN

"Everybody wants a quick fix and tries
to eat better by doing something
they think will work. All you need is
to take it one small meal at a time."

TONY GRECO

STRONG MIND LEAN BODY

The more marketers sell you on which type of diet you should do if you want to lose weight or fit a certain image that appeals to you, the more confused your body and mind get. There are just so many fads out there, all which may show a temporary result, but really do not give you a permanent solution for learning how to eat in a way that benefits your brain and body. That's what food should be intended to do, as its primary function!

The answer to how to best eat is simple, and proven.

Eat Less More Often (ELMO)

Contrary to what you may think about food, eating should be a full-time job for you. So forget the crap, and start focusing on food as the fuel your body needs to do whatever you need it to do for the day. You don't need a magic pill or a million-dollar solution—you simply need the right foods.

The next "miracle" diet is actually what's in the food you eat, not in the diet fad you could follow—but hopefully do not! Your miracle exists in:

- What you eat
- When you eat
- How much you eat

There is no need to look any further! In fact, the secret that so many people seek to find has been around for many centuries, dating back to BC times.

"Let food be thy medicine and medicine be thy food."

HIPPOCRATES, 460 BC

I remember how my parents brought this stuff from the garden to eat and that's what they said was good for the diet. Then they'd laugh at me when I'd say, "Well, oatmeal is good too." Their response—we used to feed that to the horses back in Italy. What were my parents really saying? It was a truth that is clouded for most people. It's not complicated. You need to go natural and eat from the land.

- Natural oats and grains
- Fruits
- Vegetables
- Nuts
- Green vegetables

If you remember to eat from the land as much as you can, your body is going to reward you for it. All these energy bars and sugar loaded temptations are bogus. You don't need them, and better yet, once you start weaning your body off your addiction to them you will not want them. You'll feel satisfied without them. I'm not saying you'll never cheat, but when you do, you won't feel so good about it.

THE BATTLE OF CALORIES VERSUS THE "RIGHT" FOODS

If you were to eat the proper types of foods you would be able to eat more food, more often, and not have to worry about your weight.

Imagine that you come into my office and you tell me that you eat pretty well, but you do have your chocolate and other things now and again... You only do that once in a while... It goes on and on. Those words tell me what I already know, no one is perfect. I'm sure not perfect.

You don't have to be perfect, but you have to be consistent in eating good, nutritious foods.

Striving for consistency should be your goal when it comes to your food intake.

So, if you want to lose weight there are two ways to do it.

First Way to Lose Weight

I could look at what you're doing as far as exercise and your food intake already. I diminish your calories, something I dislike doing because it is not the right solution, in my opinion. Then at the end of the week you'll go on the scale and be happy that you lost some weight, but you are likely not feeling all that great because you're hungry, going without, maybe having withdrawal headaches, etc. It is not the pleasant experience it should be.

Taking in an extra 3,500 calories a week equates to one pound of fat!

You could work out every single day and continuously fuel your engine, but what do you think would happen? Imagine if you overfill the gas tank on your car? What happens to that gas? It is going to spill out of the gas tank. If you keep eating after you're at "full," you start to wear it on your hips, on your stomach, etc. Then you start beating yourself up and don't know what's going on. And counting calories is not an easy thing to do. It takes time, time that could be spent doing better things.

If you count calories you are basically saying that you do not want to make a lifestyle change. Because you're not willing to eat differently, just less. That offers zero reward, in my opinion.

Second Way to Lose Weight

The healthy way to lose weight is to look at what you eat and when you eat it. Look at your hand. How many fingers do you have? This reminds you of why you have to eat five times a day, every 3-4 hours. The remainder of the time is when you should be in cruise mode, your body resting and preparing for the next day.

When you are resting, the nutrients you intake are feeding your muscles.

Energy expenditure happens during the remainder of the time. If you want to make sure you're moving more than you're taking in you can still lose weight and count calories, but this means you're still limiting yourself. You don't have to think in terms of limits if you think of the nutrients you intake, because all the best sources of nutrients are made of healthier fat and calories. Just because a candy bar and a piece of fish are both 300 calories, doesn't mean they are doing the same thing for you.

Micronutrients:

Micronutrients are the vitamins, minerals, trace elements, phyto-chemicals, and antioxidants that are essential for good health.

Macronutrients:

Macronutrients are the structural and energy-giving caloric components of our foods that most of us are familiar with. They include carbohydrates, fats and proteins.

You want food that provides energy throughout the body, which is where your macronutrients come in. When it comes to how you expend your energy, if you're only walking every day you're maybe expending 200 calories. It's something, but not really what will help you lose weight. When we calculate your macronutrients, you'll be better prepared to lose weight. The key is to use The Hand System.

THE HAND SYSTEM

Open your hand and look at it. You may not be able to sense it right now, but in your open hand is where the magic of ELMO exists.

When you look at your palm you see:
- An estimate of the size of how much protein you should be getting daily from a source such as chicken or turkey (or lots of vegetables if you're a vegetarian or vegan).

  Protein is essential because it keeps the muscles form getting worn and torn because of the branching reaction of amino acids. This is our own muscle.

When you look at your fist you see:
- The answer to how many veggie portions (for fiber) you should have in a day.

  You'll use this as your fuel and it'll come from vegetables, lentils, beans, and other high fiber sources.

When you look at your cupped hand you see:
- The recommended amount of carbohydrate portions for your day.

When you look at your thumb you see:
- A good suggestion for the amount of fat you should have.

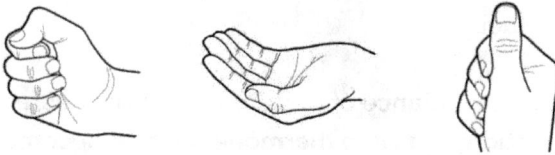

What works great with The Hand System is that your hands are proportionate to the rest of your body, which makes it easier to gauge a healthy portion without even having to entertain calories.

What is really exciting to understand about The Hand System is that it is a meal you can eat every 3-4 hours.

This is what that plate of food may look like:
- 3 to 5-ounce source of protein—a chicken breast
- A vegetable—such as two cups of asparagus, preferably steamed, sautéed in olive oil (to cover the fat)
- ½ cup rice or a baked potato

This would be an entire meal you could eat every 3-4 hours.

Before you think I'm crazy and dive into those thoughts I've often heard—I am not nuts and no, you don't need a personal chef to cook your meals. Although, if you could afford to have one to cook you this type of nutrition, why not take advantage? In an ideal world I would take a chef to cook me the right foods at the right schedule.

Train yourself to be the chef, and realize that you don't have to take a half hour to make everything from scratch all those times per day. I'll cover some options for you in a bit. But for now, realize that you need to make sure you are creating an internal alarm that reminds you that you need to eat every 3-4 hours, and that you are responsible for making sure it's the right type of fuel.

You need to have the balance of protein, carbohydrates, and fat every 3-4 hours so your body gets into thermogenesis—it becomes a furnace that keeps burning all day long.

If you've ever been around a wood fire stove that you relied on for heat, you know that every 3-4 hours you have to stoke that fire by putting logs on to fuel it to maintain the heat level you want. Your body is no different with protein. When you relate this to your body; if you're not feeding your body it turns to the muscle and reminds you that you're not fueling it. The body instinctually knows that it has to keep you warm and fueled and when no proteins or fats are present for it to burn, it will burn muscle. It refuses to shut down.

You don't want to get your body to the point where it burns muscle because then it uses fat as a security blanket.

136

There are different kinds of fat, some good and some bad.

The bad fats include:
- Trans
- Hydrogenated
- Saturated

You will find these foods in chips, frozen meals, processed foods, deep fried foods, and other junk foods. The more boxed and in the center aisles of a grocery store, the more at risk you are of choosing bad fats.

The good fats are ones that are:
- Monounsaturated
- Polyunsaturated

You will find these fats in avocados, cheese, dark chocolate, whole eggs, fatty fish, nuts, chia seeds, pure coconut oil, and extra virgin olive oil. Using these as fat sources for cooking and consumption is always going to be a better choice.

The problem with adhering to this arises in perception, because many people cannot understand that they should eat fat, especially with a weight loss goal. The reason it's necessary is that good fat is the primary fuel. When you exercise you run on glycogen and glucose. Glycogen is your fuel tank and glucose is your reserve tank. So what happens is that the body understands that it's getting fed proper amount of nutrients through The Hand System and then it starts to process them properly.

For example, if I was your chef and you needed to lose ten pounds, but you didn't move and I still fed you every three hours, you would lose anywhere from five to ten pounds. Now, you wouldn't have a lot of energy for much else because you haven't moved, but your body would start to shrink because the process of your body metabolizing those nutrients and going into thermogenesis would make you lose fat.

The good thing about this is that you get to eat a lot of food. The challenge arises if you are someone who wants your glass of wine, your ice cream, etc. What do you do then?

If this sounds like you, remember this: need and want are two different things. If you choose to have things that fall outside of this parameter, that's fine, *if* you look to another way to offset those "wants." If you want "that" and it's all that you want, you can have it. You just have to make sure that you do something to offset it. You may think, *okay, I want that glass of wine and it's acidic, so I have to go for a workout*. It doesn't get much easier than that—so don't convince yourself otherwise. You hold all the power.

In my life, I freely admit that I'm far from perfect. I eat about 90% great, and I also eat things I like that definitely do not qualify as the healthiest food for my body. But I've conditioned myself to know what comes next: I work out twice as hard to make up for it. That system works for me, and my line of work. What system can you make work for you if you want to indulge on occasion?

You should never stop yourself from living, but you should learn how to juggle.

You just have to know what to do, and that's the basics of it. There's a bit of psychology involved too, because if you are constantly denying yourself what you want, especially with food or drink because they are very social, you're going to either quit and feel like a failure or be miserable. Neither is a good option. Find a way to give yourself permission to enjoy what you wish in exchange for giving your body and mind what it needs—great nutrition and exercise.

I have seen, and live a life, in which the ELMO system works, especially when combined with The Hand System. It takes away the guess work, and allows me to focus on everything else. Like with most processes that involve change, the simpler you can make that change, the better your chances for success in changing your lifestyle to one that begins to work better for you.

Two final tips to leave you with for The Hand System are that if you do have a goal to lose weight, the two things you will want to do are:

- Eat lots of good proteins;
- And do resistance training—which is weights.

And remember:

- You do need protein, and even those who say they are on a high-protein diet often don't get enough. Protein is not necessary for only gaining muscle, but for also developing both short and long muscle fibers.
- You do need carbs. Your brain needs 150 grams a day just to function; choose complex carbohydrates because they have a slow burn and last longer over simple carbohydrates.
- You need fiber, which is not sugar.
- Healthy fats are necessary to eat.

ARE YOU CONVINCED?

It's not easy to see the value in lifestyle changes, particularly in your diet, when it seems like a tough task. You have read all of this and likely agree with what was shared. You're excited. In fact, you plan on doing it. However, if I were to come up with a companion piece to this book next week that offered one magical solution that meant you didn't have to do any of this, how quickly would your mind change? I bring this up as a last reminder to not fall for the scams. You alone have complete control over the process that will deliver you results.

12 TIPS FOR BETTER FOOD CHOICES

Ready for a shock? In order to eat better you don't have to go to the "O-word"—organic. Think of nutritional content first and foremost and you'll be great.

Here are some practical steps that you can take to begin to transition your mindset and lifestyle to one where you're doing the right thing for your body and your brain, regardless of what your goals are.

1. **Realize what your needs are.**
    When you go to the grocery store (or a great farmer's market in your area) decide which type of meat or protein you're going to have. It's important to do this first, whether you are a meat eater or not, because that is your main nutrient.

2. **Only shop the outside of the store, as much as possible.**
    Everything fresh is on the outside of the store, from flowers to fruits to produce to meats and dairy.

3. **Dine out differently.**
    It's not as impossible to eat healthier when you dine out as you may think. For example, if you want a chicken dish and the skin is on it, either ask if you can order it without that or simply set the skin aside when you get the dish. Just because it's there doesn't mean you have to eat it. (Sorry moms who say different.)

4. **Choose fresh herbs over seasoning packets.**
    Really great cuts of meat and well-prepared vegetables taste great on their own, but many people do like herbs and seasonings on these things. If you are one of these people, make sure you use fresh herbs compared to pre-packaged spices because they'll have less sodium and in many cases, also have good properties for your body.

5. **Opt for less sodium as much as possible.**
    Sodium is good for nerves, electrolytes, and muscles, but our body has 85% of what it needs on its own so avoid sodium from outside sources as much as possible.

6. **Don't choose processed or frozen foods.**
    Everything bad for you is in these processed, frozen foods, and new risks about them are constantly being uncovered. Even if they say that the meal is fortified with a certain nutrient, don't think that's the best way to get that nutrient, because it never will be. The foods on the outside aisles of your grocery store are the best way to purchase those foods if you don't grow them yourself. An additional thing about

141

frozen foods that should freak you out (at least a bit) is that part of the process of preparing them is using radiation, and the way they make them taste "flavorful," as described by those who eat them often, is sodium.

7. **Avoid eating "just to eat."**
There are a few things you should not ignore about this. First, when you are not hungry, it is okay to not eat because you are basically telling your body that you're ignoring its signals. Second, when you stop thinking about what you are eating all the time, you are likely to start eating less nutritious foods. Don't be the one who looks down at those donut crumbs and gulps, *I don't even remember eating that*.

8. **Don't be deceived by restaurant, TV, and marketing portions.**
Almost every meal you see is a way larger portion than what you actually need, especially in the US and Canada. Because of this, don't be afraid of leftovers and a little self-control, whether you're at home or out at a restaurant. Or, if you want to treat yourself to a little snack, remember a little can go a long way. The French may eat cheese every day, but it's just two fingers of cheese, not two pounds of cheese. When it comes to ice cream, it's the same thing. It's a small sized ice cream cone, not a massive cone but the perfect-sized cone much like the McDonald's vanilla cone, which is my own personal favorite cheat item. The small vanilla cone has 200 Calories and 5 grams of fat, which is awesome!

9. **Learn what proper portions are.**
    People are getting lazier all the time. There are now plates that are divided out to show what portions are and make it so people don't even have to use their brain when deciding what to put in those portion slots. Don't be afraid to have a plate without borders and know (because you're smart) how much of what foods you can have. Remember—ELMO and The Hand System.

10. **Snack smartly.**
    If you need a snack, be prepared for something that will fuel your body and help you remain committed to better nutrition. Have an apple and some walnuts, or maybe two hard boiled eggs. These are light snacks that give you the right type of longer-lasting energy, not a quick high followed by the crash-and-burn. Also realize that you should consider a "snack" a meal, because if you have something like a smoothie, you can make it so it is nutritious and fills you up. It's at times like this that I love having an Extreme Isolate 97 protein shake or a Kurabie green's shake. They taste good and they don't weigh you down.

11. **Plan ahead of time so you can pick the best foods.**
    It's much easier to eat right when you plan. This is easiest done by:

- Having a prepared grocery shopping list, focusing on proteins first.
- Making snacks ahead of time that will last you for an entire week. Protein balls are a great snack that you can make ahead of time that you can take with you on the go so you are always ready to have a good snack, not just the first thing you crave that you'd like to shove into your mouth.

• Realizing that it's easiest to avoid bad choices if you have already invested your time, energy, and resources into making a better choice more effortless.

Planning ahead is the key way to make sure you are adapting your lifestyle to achieve your fitness goals, whatever they may be. It also saves you time in the long run, which is what most people appreciate, right?

1. **Drink plenty of water.**
    Yes, you hear about drinking water all the time. I am a firm believer that you should go beyond the recommended 8 glasses of water per day and make sure you drink enough until you are always peeing clear. That is the best sign that you are taking in enough water. Also, avoid those expensive bottles of water that sell you on "energy" or certain flavors and vitamins because they really aren't as great for you as you may think. Water from a garden hose in your backyard could be more pure than many of those bottled waters. So, if you want to have some flavor in your water or get an energy boost from it, put in a teaspoon of raw honey or maple sugar—just make sure it's unpasteurized. Maple syrup, in particular, has lots of antioxidants in it. You can also try a cucumber slice or a lemon if you like.

These tips are common sense, but you do need to commit to remembering them and creating shifts in how you approach your meals every day. It's easier to do than what you may feel right now. I've eaten this way for a lot of years now and because of that, it has become second nature. That's the way it can be for you, as well. Don't think it's too hard and surrender the idea because that won't cut it if you are looking for stronger, leaner, and better results out of your life. Make all your actions count!

MAKE IT HAPPEN!

Committing to ELMO and practicing portion control take preparation to make it work out optimally. I feel this is one of the most important things you can do if you really want to make a change in your life. The way you fuel your body will determine your success in nearly all areas of your life.

To get started you can make these three things happen in your life right now—starting in this moment:

1. **Practice portion control.**
    Keeping in mind everything you've read in this chapter and the tips above, stop and think next time you are ready to dive into that big plate of food. If you're at home, create a portion that falls within The Hand System guidelines, and if you're out, either order differently so you have a lighter portion, or else have control over how much of that plate you eat at one sitting.

2. **Grocery shop the outside aisle.**
    If you always remember to choose fresh over processed, you will remain in the outside aisles of the grocery store. Create your shopping list ahead of time and if you have food choices that are on the inside aisles, evaluate what they are and why you need them. There is likely a better choice that can fulfill your needs in the outside aisles.

3. **Stay hydrated.**
    Always have water by your side to drink throughout the day, and remember the "non-golden rule": if your pee isn't clear, you need to drink more water.

"The food you eat can be either the safest and most powerful form of medicine or the slowest form of poison."

———————

ANN WIGMORE

CHAPTER 9

BELIEF IS NOT ENOUGH

"Life isn't just about the good times. It's also about the bad times—the hard times—and how you handle those. Believing they'll work themselves out isn't enough. You have to take massive action to make it happen."

————————

TONY GRECO

I t would be great if the world ran on belief, alone, and that was all it took to make things happen. This doesn't mean that belief isn't good—or important—but it is not everything you need in order to succeed at any goal you have, fitness or otherwise. Life can be hard and you need to put it all into perspective by taking a series of steps, not just one.

STEP #1: BELIEVE.

If you don't believe you can do something, you are not going to be able to do it. This is why belief is important. It's tied to your thoughts and perceptions about your outcome.

STEP #2: DO NOT JUST SAY IT, DO IT.

When it comes down to the tests that show you've done what you believed you could do, these are proven by physical actions, not just emotional commitment.

For example, when we had our martial arts school, my partner Paolo and I had really slow months. We had a yearly program and people would register for it, and it was like $800 for the Black Belt Program. What happened was that most kids and adults would register for it. Some would pay upfront and others would pay monthly. But on those months where a lot of people didn't register, the bills still came although the money didn't. And they still had to be paid. At one point, we were even 3-4 months behind on our rent.

This was when we had to commit to our belief in what we were doing. Was it worth it? To us, it was, and that meant we had to take action. I sold my 1985 Chevy Cavalier and Paolo sold a motorcycle. We put the money into the account and kept going on. That made us more committed than ever because we were more vested in our goal. This meant staying on top of the competition, keeping interest high for current students, and drawing in new students in whatever ways we could.

People who believe and don't go out there and do it are always going to have regrets later in life. I firmly believe you don't have to live with regrets.

Through all of this and focusing on add-ons for the business it kept growing because it reminded people of why they wanted to do fitness, more so than what they were doing. It was very effective. Suddenly, my commitment to the Karatecize VHS tape that led to Greco Lean and Fit

149

and so on really expanded our presence. The hard work and effort put in had taken root and began to grow and expand out, creating strength and more opportunities to continue growing what I loved and was so passionate about.

What are you doing to achieve what you want so you have no regrets?

People can have a positive life or a negative life. For me, back then one of the most major things that motivated me was not wanting to fail—myself or my family. If you believe in something, great, but you have to be strong minded in that belief that when other people are sleeping you are willing to be up and do the work, if that is what it takes. This drive is necessary for anything you want to do.

Take action by:

- Developing the discipline, conviction, and resilience you need. When other people are not doing stuff, you are.
- Remembering that if you're not the leader of the pack, your view will never change. This is something I always tell my athlete clients, because working hard to be ahead of others, especially in a competitive environment, does matter. You don't have to sell your soul or have tunnel vision to do this; you just have to go beyond your belief and into action mode.
- Determine your actions and pick the order you wish to do them in. Know your plan and work your plan, and then as you need to, adapt your plan. Just make sure you aren't reducing it because you didn't put in the time.

If you don't want to do these things, there's a good chance you either don't believe enough in what you want, or you are simply not pursuing what you should be. If you think this is the case, it's a great time to see how you've been tending to your U Seed. Is it covered in weeds or basking in the sun?

THE IMPORTANCE OF TIME

Time is running out and if you waste it you can never get it back. There is always that light at the end of the tunnel when you wake up bright and early that you are ready to make it happen. But so often, we don't pay attention.

I am more aware today about time than what I used to be because I'm in my late forties. I accept that time is running out and that means that everything I have left to accomplish needs to be committed to.

You've got to control what you can. So, assuming you're healthy and you're living a good solid life, there's a lot you can do. You have to make your time count, though, and not waste it on what you don't want to do. Focus on what you want to do and the things you can accomplish.

Everything has a season and can run its course. Even when I came to the conclusion about selling my company, I knew it was time to let go because I was ready for a new chapter. I recognized that I needed a team to uplift me and eliminate a lot of the stress in my life. This was when Andy Scott stepped in.

The resources that Andy had, as both my attorney and a sports agent, showed exactly why we have always had such a great relationship, both with me training hockey players he refers to me as their agent, and with him helping the franchise grow. He was there from location number one all the way through location 14.

When Paolo and I asked him to help us sell the franchise, he stepped into the role of investment banker, really helping us do everything we needed to sell. A goal was set to sell within one year and he got to work. He ended up making a trip to New York City to approach potential investors and ended up getting a meeting with Integrity Square, who typically didn't look at franchises as small as what I'd built. But fate was good to us and Andy Scott got a meeting with an interested party. Unfortunately, that guy left and the file was handed over to Peter Moore. At first, he was leery, but finally decided to take a trip to Ottawa with some other investors to view all the facilities. When they got there, they were impressed enough that they wanted in. And with a few key investors, the rest was history.

People like Andy Scott are a key reason why I've been able to grow my passions and business the way I have. They always saw what I wanted and helped me achieve it. So, although I make things happen, it has also taken support and efforts from key people like this.

Today, I still help but the organization is stronger than ever. It's in the hands of individuals who have the resources and talents to offer explosive growth potential, whereas I was no longer equipped to do that.

THE IMPORTANCE OF COACHING AND TEACHING

I've always enjoyed the coaching and teaching part of my career, but when it really became evident that I needed to focus on it more was when I saw the behaviors and habits of people in my classes once they left the dojo or exercise floor. They'd have this great workout and then go and have a Slurpee or a smoke, something like that. I knew that there was a problem. They were going through the motions, but not committing to fitness as a lifestyle. I wasn't sure if they didn't believe they could achieve that or just didn't know the information they needed to.

This shift to coaching and teaching from a lifestyle perspective became the heart of why fitness is a part of life—not an option, but a requirement that is holistic and encompasses the mind, body, and soul.

You must be aware of what you are doing in order to find true transformation that can change a lifestyle.

By listening to people, you can help connect them with their beliefs and the actions to make them come true. This is one of the main roles I serve as a coach and teacher. I don't just teach a movement, I teach a philosophy and a lifestyle that gives people the mindset that even on their worst day, they are better off than someone without these disciplines are on their best.

I think some of this comes from me being brought up from a tough upbringing, and that has allowed me to see how important martial arts can be to teaching all the disciplines that help guide you through all of life. Even when I won my gold medal, I would get into the ring and spar people. As their Sensei, I knew that I would not have been effective if I just ran the class. I had to participate and engage with the students in order to help them each experience their best transformation. That's one of the best things about martial arts, in the classroom it's a competition with yourself to improve and not a focus on being better than everyone else there. If you achieve a personal best, this is something to be proud of and it clearly demonstrates that you went beyond belief alone. This is so powerful, and recognizing these types of lessons can guide you through a lifetime of dedicated efforts and accomplishments. You just learn so much and in your heart you know that you are capable of doing anything you commit to.

When I help build these skills in kids or adults, I know that they are better equipped for all things that come their way. For example, if someone is going through a tough time due to maybe the death of someone close or a divorce, they understand a better approach to dealing with that situation. They may have these feelings and emotions to process through, but they also recognize the value of the outlet of exercise to help. They also learn that 90% of their efforts should be focused on the solution or the healing process.

No matter what happens, at the end of the day you have to know that you have the strength to uplift yourself, and even those around you, so you can keep going.

If you take a moment to put yourself in any scenario, you can better understand how you still have to live your life, even if something rough is happening. You can be sad or mad, but you are still alive, which means you have to be strong. Curve balls can be painful, but they can be managed if you believe you can deal with them head on.

Don't let life frustrate you! It's all perspective. Many times, putting forth the effort leads to greater appreciation. Gimme"s are worthless, but earning something never is.

One thing that I never did for my martial arts students was make it easy for them to achieve their Black Belt. They had to put in the time and commitment to learn the discipline and patience, while also realizing that even a little progress is still progress. It's not always going to be big growth and a quick reward. You just have to have the resilience to keep going and moving forward. This is part of the mindset that makes martial arts so special. The right program forces you to focus on your physical awareness, mental presence, and spiritual connection. If you develop this within yourself, you can handle anything.

RESULTS STEM FROM CONFIDENCE

I had a client once that would not even come into the center because he was embarrassed by his weight. All my coaching I did for him was over the phone, but he was still motivated because his also obese brother had recently died from a massive stroke and he didn't want that to happen to him.

At one point in this guy's life he would go through the fast food drive thru and order fifteen burgers at a time, fully loaded, and eat them in one sitting. All his outings were late at night because he was embarrassed to be seen. He'd isolated himself and then he'd received his wake-up call. He was starting at a low point, but he did want to change and his personality was one that showed he had a great heart. If he could do something for someone, he'd do it. However, the time had come where he was forced to admit that it was time for him to do something for himself.

I told him that eating was his biggest challenge and I'd call him every day to touch base with him and help coach him through his developing changes in mindset and lifestyle that he needed. What he did to help cement his desire to change is start writing a column for a local paper, *The Ottawa Citizen*. That was his way of remaining committed.

He ended up losing 150+ pounds and his life did change. He started to run and even got a government job. As these changes took hold, he felt more motivated and to this day, he's still healthy, a great basketball player, and he gets out there a lot more. What kept him going was the coaching and his column. A lot of people followed that column and gained inspiration from it. That was something beautiful about his story—he helped others gain belief that they could change through helping encourage him during his change. It extended out there, and with any authentic way to transform your life, it will spread to others and be truly helpful—unlike miracle solutions.

MAKE IT HAPPEN!

I believe that a powerful thought is fuel for action. In order to do this, you have to extend yourself beyond what you believe you can do, and actually do. There is no other way and there is no in between. These are three ways you can make this happen in your life with everything you choose to touch.

1. **Put yourself to the test.**
   Thinking "I'd like to…" followed by whatever it is that you desire is great. However, until you test it out and see if you'd really like to, it's a waste of time. Don't be one of those people who only think about what they'd want to do. Find something you'd like to try and commit to it. Maybe it's to run a marathon, learn a new skill, or to just be able to run up and down a flight of stairs without getting tired. Put yourself to the test by training for it, remembering that your attitude, diet, and movement are the three components that will make it happen.

2. **Visualize your outcomes.**

   I work with a lot of hockey players and one of the things that I always tell them is to use visualizations to see the result, and then we break it back down to the basics. I make sure they know how to do proper techniques with exercises that can help them perform better in their sport. This may be learning how to do a better squat or a proper lunge—things like that. There is so much important information in these small steps that help to condition the mind and body to cooperate with the vision they have. Maybe it's to score more goals or to have a faster hustle to the puck. Whatever it is, by breaking it down the visualization is more quickly realized.

3. **Do what it takes.**

   When you are committing to action you need to start with a plan, and then look at the plan for updates as necessary. Some steps in it may happen more quickly than you imagined, while others take longer. If it's important to you, it shouldn't matter how long it takes, so long as you keep moving forward every day. As your lifestyle transitions and you grow more committed, even the toughest days are ones where you are still willing to do what it takes.

"Knowing is not enough; we must apply.

Willing is not enough; we must do."

JOHANN WOLFGANG VON GOETHE

CHAPTER 10

INSPIRED LIFE NATURALLY & THE ROLE OF BIOIDENTICAL HORMONES

By Guest Author Dr. Joël Villeneuve, ND, Founder of RevivelifeTM Clinic

"As we go through life changes a shift occurs in our hormones. With bioidentical hormones, we now have solutions that allow us to remain more vibrant."

DR. JOËL VILLENEUVE, ND

Tony and I met years ago, as we would always come across one another at various health-related events. I quickly learned that Tony's passion for fitness was equal to mine for longevity medicine, metabolism, hormones, and nutrition. With our shared desire to help people achieve the highest performance possible for their lifestyle, it was a natural fit to collaborate. Today, Tony is the Director of Fitness & Lifestyle at RevivelifeTM Clinic in Ottawa, Ontario.

This integrated approach to wellness involves having an understanding of bioidentical hormones and their role in our lives. As it turns out, you don't have to blindly accept the changes that occur with aging. There is a great deal you can do to look and feel optimal versus "*normal*," and in a natural manner.

When you go through life changes, you may find it harder to get up in

160

the morning, have *"brain fog"* and or find that *joie de vivre* you once felt has taken a vacation.

The idea with bioidentical hormone replacement therapy (BHRT) is to offer a natural option for replenishing hormone balance so you feel rejuvenated.

WHAT HAPPENS WHEN THERE IS A HORMONAL IMBALANCE?

One of the first hormone imbalances that may occur is adrenal fatigue. This isn't a condition noted by traditional western medicine, but the impacts of an exhausted, adrenal gland develop when a person is under chronic stress, eats poorly, and/or does not get enough sleep. Because imbalances in the adrenal gland impact all hormonal systems, many symptoms begin to occur with a significant reduction in one's ability to recuperate from physical, mental or emotional stress.

There are four main phases in adrenal fatigue.

During the first *"wired"* phase, you will have an increase in the stress hormones cortisol, norepinephrine, epinephrine/adrenaline, DHEA, and blood sugar hormone insulin. Adrenaline gives you the boost to get things done and makes you feel like you just drank ten cups of coffee. However, this also causes:

1. Increased belly weight
2. Elevated cortisol levels
3. Increased anxiety

This is okay to experience occasionally, but not consistently. If you don't rest to recharge, you'll enter the second phase of fatigue—the *"wired and tired"* phase where you're alert during the day but you crash at night.

Those continued late nights and early days lead to the third phase, which is *"resistance."* In this phase the master hormones pregnenolone and progesterone are directed to produce more cortisol and thus there is a reduction of the production of sex hormones (estrogen, progesterone and testosterone). Women often become estrogen dominant, leading to irregular periods, PMS, irritability, water retention and trouble sleeping. This stage is related to higher levels of inflammation, fatigue, lack of enthusiasm, infections, and lower libido.

Ultimately, when hormonal imbalances are not addressed, it will result in the fourth phase of adrenal fatigue, which is *"burn-out."* During this time, there is a general hormone insufficiency of all hormones, including cortisol, DHEA, sex hormones, and serotonin. This leads to a risk of extreme fatigue, lack of libido, irritability, depression, anxiety, weight loss, and disinterest in the world around. Preventing yourself from getting to this stage is important, as it takes significant time to heal and significant changes to your lifestyle are required to regain balance.

When adrenal fatigue is present a thyroid imbalance often occurs as the thyroid is the back-up gland to the adrenal gland. The thyroid steps in and slows everything down to catch up.

Underactive thyroids are more commonplace than we realize, but they often go undetected because of the current diagnostic techniques.

Conditions of the thyroid are common for me to see in patients at the clinic. In today's medical community, a medical practitioner typically tests for Thyroid-Stimulating Hormone (TSH). The problem is that the range for TSH is very wide—anywhere from 0.35 milliunits per liter (mU/L) to 5 mU/L. This is what is considered *"normal."* However, our goal at the clinic is not to have you feel normal, but optimal.

Research shows that most people feel at their best when their TSH is at less than 2.0, and people start developing symptoms when it elevates higher than 2.0 including significant weight gain and fatigue.6

Everyone has their own *"optimal level"* of thyroid hormones that should be considered, more so than just the value on the lab reports. A person could be experiencing hypothyroid type symptoms for years before they ever get help. And by that time, they've had years of being tired, having digestive problems, elevated cholesterol, fertility issues and weight gain. Conducting work to find that *"optimal level"* is important work at my clinic, because if you only check for one hormone without ensuring others are good, you could be circumventing the root of the problem. It's the sum of all these components that make up the best plan of action.

Eventually, you must ask yourself: where did this all start? The answer is with your cortisol levels.

CORTISOL, SLEEP, AND YOUR DIET

When cortisol is depleted, what options do you have? This is the natural question that anyone asks once the problem has been identified. My first recommendation is to get enough rest.

Begin winding down a few hours before bedtime. You can do this by dimming the lights, which will increase the production of your nighttime hormones of melatonin and growth hormones, and decrease the production of your daytime hormones.

Normally your circadian rhythm shifts as cortisol rises first thing in the morning at about 6 AM when you see sunlight signaling the body that it's time to rise in a more energized state. Cortisol then begins to fall at about 6 PM, when the sun begins to set signaling the body that it's time for sleep.

With a chronic cortisol imbalance, am cortisol may be so low so that one cup of coffee is no longer enough to get you going and you then need two or three.

When a person has a chronic cortisol imbalance it is usually a deficiency and it takes quite a while to get the level higher during the daytime.

This leads to running on adrenaline all day and when you try to sleep, you run into problems. Your cortisol has shifted, and it is too high. It's a debilitating cycle. Eventually, you will either fall asleep or become so tired that you fall asleep, but cannot stay asleep. You keep waking up every 90 minutes or so, never being able to go into deep REM sleep.

Part of restoring balance involves shifting that cortisol pattern by developing better pre-bedtime habits. You need to be able to calm down and relax at the right times, which is best done through diet, essential oils, and adaptogenic herbs.

Along with rest, you must address your diet to regain control. This is such an important topic, and I believe so strongly in it, that I wrote an entire book about it, called *Power Foods 101*. Knowing how to choose and prepare the best foods to give you a chance for your best performance in life. A power foods menu is important because of these benefits of being:

- Anti-inflammatory
- Nutrient dense
- Easy to digest
- Whole foods

Additionally, these power foods are rich in phytonutrients that offer a health action including helping to reduce the risk of cancer.

The types of food we intake can be either our greatest asset to a stronger mind and lean body, or else the resistance to achieving our ideal level of peak performance.

With proper rest and power foods being addressed, the next thing you want to increase is healthy fats to provide the body's preferred source of brain fuel. The best and easiest source for healthy fats to include daily is extra virgin coconut oil (EVCO). When choosing a coconut oil, make sure that it is not refined because it will reduce the effectiveness of the medium change triglyceride (MCT), which is what gives coconut oil the beneficial properties our body needs.

Another good source of healthy fats is avocado or alphabet fruit, thanks to all the nutrients that it contains from vitamin A to zinc.

Healthy fats also help to absorb micronutrients, which is another key aspect to focus on in your diet.

By eating healthy forms of foods that promote micronutrients and minerals we can fuel the various chemical reactions that produce energy.

Most of these micronutrients come from fresh vegetables—the darker the green, the better. Three great sources include:

- Kale
- Spinach
- Arugula

Enjoy these greens raw or steamed. Just do not overcook them so you break down the properties that are most beneficial to you.

Other vegetables can offer these micronutrients, but in lower concentrations. By choosing dark greens first, you get the best bang for your buck, because in addition to minerals they provide:

- Fiber
- Chlorophyll
- Calcium

Healthy fats and dark greens are necessary for creating the energy that helps you last the entire day. It will always beat sugar as a source of fuel!

Avoid processed sugars because they interfere with cortisol levels.

Healthy fats also reduce cravings and maintain energy. This is why you should avoid the spikes that come with processed sugar. Focus on natural sweeteners, which include:

- Fresh fruit
- Maple syrup
- Raw honey

Small amounts of these natural sweeteners offer a better defense against those crash-and-burn moments that sugar spikes bring. That *"quick fix"* is no longer necessary if your body gets enough healthy fat.

When focusing on balancing cortisol, it is also important to intake high quality protein.

To get the best protein sources, three great options include:

- Flaxseeds: ¼ cup= 8 grams
- Buckwheat: ½ cup = 12 grams(gluten-free)
- Hemp seeds: 3 Tbsp. = 10 grams

Protein becomes even more critical to a diet if you are someone who likes to exercise and train hard. Replenishing your protein levels becomes challenging in these situations. You should evaluate energy before deciding to train hard. I suggest:

- If your energy is 5-out-of-10 or higher, it's okay to exercise.
- If your energy is less than 5-out-of-10, you should rest, because your body is indicating you need it.

Another note about exercise has to do with growth hormone. Exercise is one of the largest contributors to growth hormone release. This ties it to the amount of sleep you get. When it comes to sleep, the amount required for an adult varies a bit, but averages out to eight hours of sleep per night to operate at a peak performance level during the day. The highest production of growth hormone takes place just a few hours after you fall asleep.

Growth hormone production lessens when one is obese. Since weight gain can happen when cortisol production is out of balance, your cortisol balance becomes intricately connected to growth hormone.

Growth hormone impacts our ability to perform psychologically and physically by impacting:

- The aging process
- Brain function
- Energy

There's so much to take in, but in the end, know that rest is always your priority. By getting enough sleep and exercise, while also consuming power foods, healthy fats, micronutrients, and the proper amounts of proteins, your hormone levels become much easier to manage. You begin to experience the benefits of the proper amount of energy (received in the proper way) to excel at your day.

ESSENTIAL OILS AND ADAPTOGENIC HERBS FOR RELAXATION

Essential oils offer health benefits to you that can help your body gently transition into a relaxed state toward the end of your day. Adaptogenic herbs can also offer many of the same benefits by helping your body adapt to and promote wellness within it.

With essential oils for promoting calmness and relaxation, look to:

- Lavender
- Myrrh
- Frankincense
- Bergamot

All these oils naturally reduce cortisol and inflammation, while also promoting greater sleep quality and digestion.

There are several ways to receive the benefits of essential oils, with the two most popular being to place them on your pulse points or to use an infuser.

The adaptogenic herbs that work wonderfully for relaxation and reducing cortisol during your sleeping hours include:

- Ashwagandha
- Rhodiola rosea
- Ginseng
- Holy basil
- Certain medical mushrooms, such as reishi and cordyceps

These herbs and essential oils can be aids to restoring balance. It does take time – an average of 12 weeks – to restore a normal sleep cycle that is optimal for hormonal balance and to restore the quality of your life. During this time, lifestyle adjustments should be addressed that will help support your efforts.

TAKE THE iENERGY HEALTH & HORMONE QUIZ

The following questionnaire is designed to increase your knowledge and awareness of your overall health, and to highlight potential areas of concern. For each symptom you experience often, score 1 point. If you experience any of the symptoms frequently or in bold, score 2 points. The maximum score for each category is 10 points. Many symptoms occur more than once as they can be related to multiple imbalances. Put your total score in each section if the Your Score Box.

If you score more than 5 in any category, consider following up for the proper lab tests and evaluation.

5 STEPS TO OPTIMIZING YOUR MIND AND BODY

When you are changing a lifestyle to create the changes that give you a higher level of performance, you need a combination of information and a strategy to act upon.

By this point you've likely speculated about which obstacles you may be facing in regards to your hormonal balance. Truthfully, testing for imbalances is the only way to really assess the situation. From my position, I have seen the most incredible changes take place after tests revealed the starting point for recovery.

However, there are things you can do—starting today. Here are 5 steps I'd like to share with you to help guide you to more energy, vitality, and abundance.

DIGESTION

- ☐ Eat at your desk or on-the go
- ☐ Bloating
- ☐ Pain
- ☐ Diarrhea
- ☐ Constipation
- ☐ Acne, Eczema &/or Psoriasis
- ☐ Fatigue
- ☐ Lack of glow... hair, skin, nails

_____ TOTAL SCORE

LIVER

- ☐ Sluggish
- ☐ Sensitive- medications, perfumes, alcohol
- ☐ Aches & Pains
- ☐ Weight gain
- ☐ Headaches
- ☐ Allergies
- ☐ Lack of glow... hair, skin, nails

_____ TOTAL SCORE

INSULIN

- ☐ Low energy, especially mid-day
- ☐ Poor memory
- ☐ Cravings
- ☐ Frequent colds, flus, allergies
- ☐ Weight gain-belly

_____ TOTAL SCORE

CORTISOL

- ☐ Insomnia
- ☐ Stressed out
- ☐ Tired but Wired
- ☐ Low energy
- ☐ Foggy brain
- ☐ Cravings
- ☐ Frequent colds, flus, allergies
- ☐ Weight gain-belly
- ☐ Frequent injuries

_____ TOTAL SCORE

THYROID	PROGESTERONE	ESTROGEN	TESTOSTERONE
☐ Low energy	☐ Irritable	☐ Low mood	☐ Low energy
☐ Dry skin, hair or nails	☐ Stressed Out	☐ Dry/wrinkled skin	☐ Low self confidence
☐ Hair loss	☐ Insomnia	☐ Low energy	☐ Loss of muscle tone
☐ Loss of outer margin of eye brows	☐ Water retention	☐ Poor memory	☐ Weight gain-belly
☐ Hoarse voice	☐ Frequent periods	☐ Insomnia	☐ Low libido
☐ PMS	☐ Heavy & painful periods	☐ Hot flashes	
☐ Constipation	☐ PMS	☐ Head aches	
☐ Weight gain-generalized	☐ Headaches	☐ Heart palpations	
		☐ Vaginal dryness	
		☐ Weak bladder	
_____ TOTAL SCORE	_____ TOTAL SCORE	_____ TOTAL SCORE	_____ TOTAL SCORE

1. **Implement ideas in small, bite-size pieces.**
   Slow steps that lead to lifestyle changes you can adhere to is a key to your success. For example, if you need to eat better, start with breakfast and build from there.

2. **Receive coaching to help you shift your perspective.**
   Even when you are making changes for the better, you're going to face good days and challenging days. A lifestyle or nutrition coach can help you change your perspective and address any emotional components, as necessary. These professionals are an excellent source of support!

3. **Set meaningful goals.**
   By keeping yourself engaged in your own learning and growth process, you can find success in things that interest you and inspire you to try to grow upward every day. When we achieve goals, we gain confidence about our ability to succeed at what we set our mind to.

4. **Reward yourself.**
   A reward is something you give yourself to celebrate a success. If you were successful at shifting your breakfast, look at how you can celebrate that. You may really love a certain herbal tea—decide to purchase that to give yourself a little treat. Or if it works with your budget, go for that massage.

5. **Have small retreats to nature, as necessary.**
   If you ever feel the need to get away and clear your mind, as well as liberate your body from stress, concerns, or even an overall feeling of sluggishness, do not hesitate to turn to nature. Just go out into the woods and enjoy a meditative walk, or simply take in the scents and

sounds around you. Nourish yourself in the sunshine and breathe in the fresh air. This does wonders for emotional balance, as well resets the body for better sleep, food choices, and hormonal balance.

In my work and life, I have a simple goal, which is to inspire health, naturally. Life is busy and as a result we sometimes falter on making the best choices. Life is a journey and being optimal mentally and physically is a continuous process—one that is necessary for a stronger mind and lean body. Never abandon doing what it takes to be better...because it is worth it.

ABOUT DR. JOËL VILLENEUVE, ND

Naturopathic Dr. Joël Villeneuve, ND is a North American expert in Longevity Medicine, Metabolism, Hormones and Nutrition. She has recently been awarded the "Lifetime Achievement Award" for her contribution to health and wellness. She is recognized for her roles as an integrative doctor, author (www.powerfoods101.com), health program developer (Maximized Metabolix, High Performance Lifestyle & Be Lean,) TV & media personality, educator, and national speaker with over 25 years of experience in the Health Care Industry.

Dr. Joël is the founder, clinical director, and CEO of The *Revivelife™ Clinic*, which is one of the region's largest providers of integrated health services, working in alliance with medical doctors, businesses, the fitness industry and government bodies to promote optimal wellness. Dr. Joël has supported thousands of patients to optimal health with her vision is to inspire vitality, balance, and empowerment in all.

She has trained with world leaders in their fields, including Dr. Neal Barnard, MD leader in Nutritional Medicine; Dr. Caldwell Esselstyn, MD expert in

Cardiovascular Medicine; Dr. Thierry Hertoghe, MD, international hormone expert, including his work with Suzanne Somers; and Dr. Erika Schwartz, MD, bio-identical hormone doctor. www.drjoel.ca.

CHAPTER 11

BE FIT, LIVE BETTER

"There is not a single part of your life that is not impacted by your level of fitness. If you really want to live a better life you have to be fit."

TONY GRECO

There are a lot of things in this world that are hard to access, but fitness *is not* one of them. It's everywhere around you and all you need to have is a body in order to do the movements. And even if your body isn't working great for you when you begin, it can still start doing some work for you to become better.

Many people have crazy schedules and the reason they are not doing what they want is that they don't do regular workouts.

Understand that if you're not doing fitness, you are a weirdo. Honestly, you are, and this isn't the time for me to avoid being blunt when I tell you that. You need to do it. It's not that you should picture yourself being a fitness model or even think you have to go to that level, but you need to go to a higher level than where you are at if you currently don't apply the disciplines of fitness into your life.

Again, these disciplines are:

- Moving the body
- Igniting the mind
- Fueling your body properly
- Thinking and acting positively to achieve your goals

For these reasons, fitness *must* be a part of your life—no exceptions. It's the fertilizer to your U Seed.

IT STARTS WITH YOUR STATE OF MIND

The number one reason most people give about not exercising is that "they don't have time." Stop! This is not the case. If you were to be honest, the answer would be: I choose to not make time. Big difference!

Fitness is a part of life. You don't have a choice because in the end it all comes down to LIFE. Do you want one or not?

Whether you are at your desk, at the park, or in the mall, you can participate in some type of fitness. You only need 20 minutes a day or a special location to start making an impact. And you don't need equipment to do this, either, because body weight exercises are the most effective exercises anyway. So even if you're away on vacation or a trip, you can pack an elastic band in your suitcase or use the furniture around you to do dips, some types of pushups, or leverage yourself for sit-ups. There is always something you can do! And these are great workouts, as well.

One of the things I do is design a five-minute workout. It's simple and I can do it anywhere I need to, and with my schedule it is necessary sometimes because while I am completely passionate and committed to helping everyone realize that fitness is a part of life, not an option, I am a busy guy. Sometimes there are back to back meetings, and I do have to travel a lot. But I never—absolutely never—skip out on movement because I know that with it, I am not only doing what I need to do better, but I am not being a hypocrite and telling other people to do something that I don't practice myself.

179

With these five-minute exercises I focus on two areas:

- Posterior—muscles on the back side of the body
- Anterior muscles—muscles on the front side of the body

By focusing on this you can do exercises where you pull and you push, which would be doing a combination of something like a push-up and then a chin-up (because you push and pull both). You can also do squats and lunges. And I will do this stuff whenever I need to. Just look around you and see the potential. Remember the reference to HALO? If I'm at a park, I'll use that park bench to step up and down, and doing that feels good and my body knows that I'm not ignoring it. It knows how to process when I move, but would have no idea what to do if I wasn't moving. Even way back when I had my jaw broken, I continued to do everything I could for fitness that was manageable with it wired shut.

There are so many different things you can do, and even mentioning a single excuse of why you can't do something should be unacceptable to you.

If you physically can't move, that's different, of course. But you can still do some exercises. I have a client that can have a great upper body workout that's in a wheelchair. Being handicap isn't an excuse. Nothing is an excuse!

In my business, I often see how people are unhappy with their life. Far too many people, and this often happens because they are too focused on having material things, making it so they don't really realize what it is they want and need. This is when you have to ask yourself: do I want it or do I need it? That can help get you on track. And what happens next is a series of excuses, and really it comes down to this:

CHAPTER 11: BE FIT, LIVE BETTER

Laziness leads to pain.

Two hundred years ago you wouldn't be docile. I'll refer to my parents again and the amount of physical work they did. I remember my mom saying that today's generation could never outdo the work she did. She would get up at 4:30 in the morning and get to the garden, start picking tomatoes, and then go into the kitchen and stew them or do whatever else with them. She'd go straight until 2:00 in the afternoon, or so. That's crazy. Today you could never get a fifteen or sixteen year old to do that, just standing there and not being distracted. The point I'm making is not about the generational gap, it is that people who do a lot of physical stuff can outlast most of the current generations 20X over. It's sad, really.

I want to get to these kids and adults who cannot keep pace with what used to come naturally to older generations, and let them know that with thirty to forty-five minutes of exercise a day, they will have such a better life. This means:

- More energy
- More joy
- More mobility
- More experiences
- More successes

Don't you want more of all the right things?

The more you use your body, the better it gets. If your mind and your body are connecting, you are connecting with more. It doesn't have to be more complex than that. If the pathway to more is fitness, why not do it?

181

Everybody wants more of something. I know they do because everyone I talk about this topic with admits as much.

GENETICS VERSUS YOUR INITIATIVE

When it comes to your health, 80% is what you eat and only 20% is genetics. So saying that I'm naturally overweight because I'm Italian, from Eastern Europe, or whatever becomes an excuse. You can be fit if you are from these types of areas and don't have to fall into some stereotype that gives you a reason to be lazy or make another excuse about why you are not the way you claim you'd like to be.

Genetics will never outweigh the choices you make regarding:

- What you eat and how you fuel your body
- The movements and exercises you do every day

These two factors make up your results, not your genetics.

The hard work and commitment to being your best "self" is always a worthy pursuit.

What genetics may impact is that you can never have the shape of butt you'd like or the size of bone structure you think is ideal, but you can't worry about those things. They are not for you. Just worry about what God has given you being taken care of properly.

I believe one of the biggest problems that people who want to blame genetics face is that they really do not eat as properly as they claim to. They believe they know it all, but they really don't. If you've fallen into this category in the past, remember the ELMO chapter, because that really lays out the blueprint for you.

A few signs that you may not know what you are eating can be found by looking at the labels. If there are ingredients that you don't know what are and that sound manmade, you really don't know what you're eating. There's a reason that the food on the outside aisles of the grocery store don't need to have an ingredients label on them, for the most part, and it's because they aren't filled with manmade ingredients. They are from nature, and as close to what nature intended them to be that you can get (minus pesticides, of course).

FINDING YOUR BEST SOLUTIONS

Your life, your body, your mind, and your energy are all reliant on how you exercise and eat—and how you solve problems when you see them arise. By now you should know that I find exercise to be the solution for:

- Avoiding medications
- Having less stress
- Feeling better emotionally and mentally
- Achieving the goals you set your mind to

But now and again, life does throw you something that you have to deal with. Finding the best solution becomes critical at this point. Take me, for example. I might have a headache, which I get now and again, because I'm just holding so much thought. My first solution in this situation is never to go for the aspirin and take one to cure the headache, or lie down and take a nap. I chose to work out and work the headache out of my system. Without fail, this solution works every time. The headache disappears and all the thoughts are more aligned and clearer.

It's not just headaches that get better. Having a good workout can be a cure all for a great many things. I work out with a group of buddies three times a week, and without fail, someone always mentions how they really need their workout that day. It's now inherently understood that when you exercise you find a solution to most any problem you may have, especially ones of attitude. And even if the root problem is severe—say finances, for example—your attitude dictates the solution.

A good workout is every bit as effective as any drug that might relax you for the next 6-8 hours.

When you do things for yourself you naturally feel more alive. I strongly recommend that everyone do this for themselves. If you feel the headache coming on, go into action. If the stress and tension are mounting up, release it by exercising. Regardless of what it is that you decide to do, just make sure it's active. Even taking a walk or breathing in deeply is better than taking a pill to solve a problem. Your best solutions are in your movements during these times.

TIP

I've learned to be proactive in solving these situations in my life by simply excusing myself for whatever amount of time I can to go and do movement to start the process of healing my mind, attitude, whatever. I recommend you grow comfortable doing the same thing, because a bit of time spent on your well-being right when it's discovered will help you be more productive and in a better state-of-mind later.

WHAT CAN YOU AFFORD?

In my profession, I really cannot afford to be sick. I'm sure the same is true for you, as well. So think of the job that you do. If you don't have your health, you can't produce the results that your employer needs you to do, or if you are self-employed, those tasks that you know you are responsible to do. Because of this, you cannot afford to be sick.

If you're not eating right, you're not healthy, and you're setting yourself up to get sick, you are not going to be able to do anything you want. Can you really afford that?

This extends beyond work. Would you rather:

- Go to your grandchildren's music recital or sit home because you don't have the energy to attend it?
- Go on that hiking adventure or stay back because you know you can't make it?

- Spend a day with your friends in the city having fun, or have to go back to your hotel room because you grow exhausted quickly?
- Play catch with your kids in the backyard or sit in a chair and watch because it hurts to put your hustle on?
- Hold on to something in order to pick something up you dropped or just be able to kneel down and pick it up?
- See any situation as manageable or let it stress you out and ruin your mood?
- Look in the mirror and see commitment, or look into the mirror and condemn yourself for what you haven't done?

All these things matter and make an impact in your life. This is why fitness is—and will always be—necessary, not optional.

MAKE IT HAPPEN!

Your life is so much more than waking up and making it through another day. Every experience you have helps to define what your life is and who you are. There are going to be challenges, but they don't have to be in charge of your results—ever. By taking some time to be more aware of yourself and the lessons that exist all around you, great things will happen.

Today is the day to make good decisions by taking a few initiatives. You have the solutions.

1. **Be aware when you're off balance.**
   You have to find the courage and your own way to step aside when you know that something's happening that is not good for you. The headache, for example. Step away and find a way to exercise or

move for a while so you can change the tide and then get back to what you want/need to do, and do it better.

2. **Talk to older people and ask them what they'd do differently.**
    This is one of my most favorite activities to do. I have a friend that owns some nursing homes and when I go visit the people in there I know that I have access to some of the best wisdom. One of the questions I like to ask most often is: "If you would have known one thing when you were younger, what would it have been?" Most often the response involves that they would have taken better care of themselves. Hindsight may be enlightening, but it is certainly not comforting, which is why you need to take action now.

3. **Visualize yourself as a healthy person aging gracefully.**
    As you know, you're aging every day, but how you age is something you can have a great deal of control over. Visualize yourself aging gracefully and see what that feels and looks like to you, according to your definition. Do you want to be active, be able to have adventures, and look and feel younger than your birth certificate says you are? If that sounds great, start making sure you turn into that visualization.

"Identify your problems, but give your power and energy to solutions."

TONY ROBBINS

CHAPTER 12

7 TIPS FOR FINANCIAL SUCCESS

By Guest Author, **John Bahen**, *Vice President and Investment Advisor, Momentum Wealth Management, a part TD Wealth Private Investment Advice*

"Being successful financially is similar to being successful mentally and physically. You must do things in the proper fashion to get the best results."

———————

JOHN BAHEN

Tony's name is one that has been familiar to me for a long time. Although we were on opposite sides of the football in high school, the word was already out about his fierce competitiveness and determination. When I finally got to know Tony as an adult, it was when my sons, and wife Susan, started to take karate at one of Tony's dojos. Everything about his life philosophies resonated with me, and as a father, husband, and former soldier, I loved what the program offered. Being there on those days when my sons and wife earned their black belts was special for me. They'd set goals and worked diligently to achieve them and I witnessed how that return paid off.

Life really is about goals and accomplishments. In order to make these experiences better, being financially fit is an important part of the equation. Not to state the obvious, but money is a necessity—you must have it to live on now and to eventually retire. It's necessary, so making sure you do whatever you can to avoid financial stress and distress becomes important. I understand how this can be challenging for people at times, which is where the services of the right financial advisor come into play. It is hard to maximize your potential without the help of someone who is involved in how the market and money works full-time. You cannot master what you do not fully understand, and most people look at financial news and don't see a whole lot of clarity in the headlines. There are often contradictions from story to story, and then there are those fear-mongering headlines. They create confusion, even for the most logical and research-oriented person.

This is where I come in. I help people make better choices.

Through my military service, I learned how to handle a stressful situation in a logical and efficient manner. I apply that learning to the daily stress of the marketing order to make smarter investment decisions.

There is a lot of information that you need to understand, at least on a basic level, and that is what I want to share with you in these 7 tips. The goal is that you will be more grounded and, as a result, create a stronger plan-of-action for your financial wellbeing, knowing that the markets are still the best tool to help you achieve your goals and grow your investments.

TIP #1: MANAGING EMOTIONS

Can you guess what the number one challenge is for most people when it comes to their response to their own finances? It's their emotions. This often plays a more significant role in poor decisions, even more so than a lack of knowledge, or an inability to visualize how all the steps taken toward financial wellness today lead to the bigger outcome for tomorrow.

If you remember that money really is math, not emotion, it becomes easier to dive into taking the proper actions in the right manner.

This is one of the greatest benefits to having the right financial partner on your side, because when you develop a relationship that is based on the facts of your specific situation – and not assumptions or "hot trends" – you gain balance. The market is known to give you rewards quickly and take them away quickly, too, if you let emotions play a part in dictating your decisions.

If this is your challenge, make sure you take initiative and create a plan that will allow your emotions not to be in charge of your finances.

TIP #2: IT'S ALL ABOUT THE MATH

On the other side of emotions is math. Math is all about logic, which makes it quite brilliant. The strategy that I use with clients is based on quantitative analysis, which means that I focus on the application of math and statistical methods for guiding clients to better investment choices. It has proven to be a successful formula and by removing emotions and opinion from investing, stronger decisions can be made. In my life and career, I can tie much of my military discipline back to relying on math. That period taught me a great deal about how to view a situation most optimally and effectively. For you, it is important to ensure that:

- You invest in good companies with positive earnings momentum
- Be purposeful in making sure investment decisions are made for a reason based on earnings
- Keep personal and opinion-based analysis and politics out of your financial fitness decisions

My firm utilizes a strict earnings analysis model to analyze which companies we will own. We run all companies through the model and after the analysis is done perhaps 30 individual stocks make the portfolio. That is how we know if the company is good enough to be owned by us. It's based on math (earnings) and we do not:

• Care what the CEO says they will be doing in the future
• Go on plant tours
• Make short term predictions

Instead, we:

• Care about the company's balance sheet
• Care that the company's earnings are higher than last quarter and heading in the right direction

And whenever we do not like the direction a company is headed, we sell immediately. When we like the direction they are going, we buy, or continue to hold.

Take this example: you buy into a company that has great prospects, but then something changes. Maybe something goes wrong causing the earnings to drop. If you bought the stock at $10 and now it's trading for $8, what do you do? Some may want to ride it out and "see if it rebounds." But really, it's most logical to sell that stock at $8 and move it to another opportunity where it will go up to $12, and not go down to $6. It's all predicated on numbers. If you are holding a stock that has negative earnings you not only have the risk of losing value on the holding, but you are losing the time where that money could have been in a company with positive earnings that could be increasing in value. You never get that time back. If you are not willing to put new money into a stock you should not be holding it with old money.

A good portfolio is determined by what you sell, more so than what you buy.

Over time, and with a math-focused investment strategy, you can begin to use a system that will allow you to make investment decisions in the proper manner. This discipline leads to good habits that will stem into all areas of finance in your life, making it an important aspect of your personal outcomes.

TIP #3: UNDERSTANDING THE IMPORTANCE OF DISCIPLINE IN INVESTING

I spend a lot of time with the clients talking about the importance of discipline in investing. Why do we buy and why do we sell? Being comfortable with the discipline and process is important to creating a successful relationship with me in an advisory capacity. It is also imperative for clients to have confidence in the discipline in order to achieve their goals. Through this, you can avoid those opinion traps and reduce your risk of:

- Being vulnerable to market hype
- Over-focusing on the short-term, while under-focusing on the long-term

Let me share some insight with you about over-focusing on the short-term. So many people commit to thinking short-term with the market, but would never do so in other important areas of their life. Can you imagine going home every single day and seeing the price of what your home was worth that day on the front door? Wouldn't that drive you crazy? I know some people who look at their portfolios every day, and frankly, it creates unnecessary anxiety. I don't even look at my own portfolio daily because I do not have to, as I have confidence in the strategy of investing in companies that are making money and proving themselves in the market.

Discipline also involves never relying on predicting the future. However, you can rely on this:

If you don't sell your losers, you're going to end up with a whole bunch of losers.

Everything comes back to discipline and using it to find good companies that are making money. We are always aware of this when we evaluate clients' portfolios. This evaluation is necessary for the work of an advisor. And you can be rest assured that any advisor who is truly successful will never guide you to invest in something that they would not put their hard-earned money into themselves. It wouldn't make sense or cents.

TIP #4: ANTICIPATE THE UNEXPECTED

None of us want bad things to happen or to experience negative disruptors, but they do happen. There is always going to be a war going on somewhere, and terrorist attacks and climate issues are becoming commonplace. Bear markets will come and go, and a political comment is going to send the markets into a tailspin on occasion. None of this can be controlled by you.

You can only control one thing—what you own.

As an investor, if you just own good companies that are making money quarter after quarter you'll do well. On the flip side, if you invest in companies that have negative earnings you won't. All you can do as an investor is strive to have the strongest portfolio. Companies with strong positive earnings weather the storm.

When it comes to the "waiting for the right time strategy," I have a firm belief: timing the market is a waste of time, as the unexpected can happen at any time. And when it does, the markets will usually respond to the disruption. It becomes the headline, and therefore it feels more important to your portfolio than it is. This brings us back to emotions and managing their involvement in your investments. For example, if some world leader sends a Tweet out that gets everyone talking and rolling with their opinions about it, it really does have only a minimal chance of impacting your portfolio if you stick to companies with positive earnings.

In the summer of 2016 we saw this come into play when the UK voted to leave the European Union. The London and German exchanges dropped almost instantly because of it. Yet, if you live in the UK you're still going to eat, own a home, drive a car, buy food, take your prescriptions, etc. Not much changes in your day-to-day life, even in "big headline" events.

Most of the economy is made up of people living and going about their daily business.

The reality is that people will continue to consume for the most part in a normal fashion and eventually the market will regulate itself again. In the end, good companies continue to do well and bad companies eventually go away. The market always figures itself out.

TIP #5: UNDERSTAND YOUR ACCEPTABLE RISK LEVELS

The level of risk we can take on is dependent on several factors, including:

- Wealth
- Age
- Comfort level
- Lifestyle

We all have different needs. One aspect of my business is I meet people from a lot of different backgrounds and successes. Everyone is little unique. We work with clients and go through a process to find out what's important to them and what they really need. You have to understand the family, it's everything. To help with this process, we provide full financial plans for our clients, and we stay updated on any changes that have taken place, which could potentially impact investment strategies. A few things that may impact an investment strategy include: having a child; sale of a business or asset; or, income adjustment.

Helping people find the right portfolio strategies that fit those needs is rewarding. Some clients are comfortable with the volatility, some aren't. It really comes down to individual preference and what you desire to achieve...what you wish to attain.

Professionally and personally, I have a lot of faith in the equity market. On the flip side, I am not one to suggest high risk investments to my clients (for obvious reasons.) Stable, good results are continuously reached through focusing on quality large-cap portfolios.

TIP #6: PAY YOURSELF FIRST

A message that I have shared with my sons is one that I believe everyone needs to share. "You've got to pay yourself first because no one else is going to do it for you." This refers to planning for the future, but also in how you budget for your day-to-day life.

When I was young, I didn't have a lot of money, but I did have the discipline to systematically save. This approach never failed me and all those times when I chose to take a pass on something I "wanted in the moment," I had no regrets later on. Life is meant to be enjoyed and to experience fun activities with friends and family. The best way to make sure you can do that is to pay yourself first.

Don't try to be further ahead in the game than your situation shows you really are, because that will lead to falling behind. And once you're behind, it's hard to get caught back up. Through remembering to divest yourself of emotion and opinion, while sticking to disciplined efforts, you can create the good habits that help your portfolio grow.

TIP #7: PLAN FOR YOUR LEGACY

Estate planning is a big part of our business and extremely important to your life. Having a team working for you that can evaluate your finances in conjunction with changing economies and markets is an optimal way to grow your wealth. Plus, what you have built up over the years is important. You want to ensure you're taking steps to:

- Protect assets
- Minimize taxes
- Provide for your loved ones

With constantly changing laws and guidelines, it takes a team of experts to really put the legacy plan together that will best fit your needs. These experts specialize in:

- Estate trusts
- Wills
- Allocations to family members
- Specific criteria that must be met
- Distribution

Ideally, a successful family should be able to maintain their wealth over generations by doing good planning and adapting a pro-growth mindset. Through setting up parameters on how funds are to be invested, allocated, and even spent, you can ensure this legacy continues. In my case, many of my clients are now generational. I started with the grandparents, moved on to the parents, and am now working with the kids.

FINANCIALLY FIT FOR LIFE

Just like you invest in your own physical and emotional wellbeing, you need to invest in your financial health.

These seven tips have given you an overall concept and plan for how you should consider looking at your finances. When people do the proper financial planning and take those right steps they really can experience so much joy—not only after they retire but through that process. Stress about money is common in far too many peoples' lives and it is hard to enjoy your life when stress sets in.

Know that today, regardless of where you are at financially, you have the potential to make smarter and wiser choices when it comes to your financial fitness. A commitment to change starts with what you decide to do today—right now. Maybe it's time to align yourself with an advisor that can best help you navigate all the details of the markets, as there are many, or it is remembering to rigorously adhere to a budget. Either way, you are meant to live a life that is filled with meaning and happier, healthier experiences. Just make sure you do all you can do to make that happen.

ABOUT JOHN BAHEN

Raised in the Ottawa area, John attended Carleton University and served in the military for nine years with the Cameron Highlanders of Ottawa as an Infantry Soldier. John graduated from Carleton University in 1991. In that same year started his financial services career with MetLife Canada. John attained Rookie of the Year Honors, and became the youngest Branch Manager in Canada in 1994 at the age of 25.

In 1997, John chose to become a full-service investment advisor focusing on building long-term wealth for his clients by choosing quality investments focused on positive earnings using a disciplined mathematical approach. Since 2007 John has been a multiple TD Wealth Merit Award Advisor which represents the top 5% of advisors in Canada. In 2008, John was appointed a Vice President of TD Wealth Private Investment Advice. In 2016 John partnered with Gordon Srdoc, VP and Investment Advisor, and formed Momentum Wealth Management within TD Wealth Private Investment Advice.

A combination of academic strength, experience, and a military background allows John to deal with the daily stress of the market in a calm, disciplined, and efficient manner.

Outside of the office, John enjoys spending time with his wife Susan and their two sons, Cameron and Colin. John is an avid outdoorsman, hockey and tennis player.

Visit http://advisors.td.com/john.bahen/index.htm to learn more.

AFTERWORD

"Life comes down to the choices
you make. You're either going
to give up or get going."

TONY GRECO

Everything related to fitness as a solution to most of life's problems is something that excites me. Every time I have an opportunity to connect with someone about this powerful message I get excited, and I am very grateful to you for reading this book. I hope you took away from it what I wished to give you. That means so much to me on many levels—it's one of my marks for success. I truly believe everyone has the potential to transform their lives through taking on a new perspective and realizing that they have a U Seed inside them that's eager and willing to bust free.

You can have—and do require—these 9 components to create a complete and balanced life:

· Optimal health
· A positive self-image
· An abundance of love
· Success with your finances and career
· A safe and stimulating personal environment
· Mental clarity and focus
· A connection to spirituality
· Play and fun

What choices are you going to make so this can happen for you? You need to believe in yourself to achieve these things, not anybody else. They can't do it for you. No matter what you struggle with or want to change in your life, only you can start the actions that lead to that transformation you desire. I can't do it for you. I can coach you and guide you, but only you can inspire yourself to take action.

You need to:

· Go for your own "gold medal" victories
· Nourish and grow your U Seed
· Commit to staying in motion
· Cut out the noise and stay focused
· View fitness as the new medicine—it's better than a pill all day, every day

- Know who you are to determine what you want
- Desire to win
- Ignite your brain so it is stimulated and constantly learning
- Engage in better ways to eat using ELMO and The Hand System
- Understand why balanced hormones are essential to graceful aging and being your best self
- Be fit so you will live better in all areas of your life
- Practice financial fitness
- Go beyond belief and take massive action on your dreams and goals

Make it happen!

At times it takes just a single shot of momentum to begin doing things that are so incredible that they extend beyond what you set up as a goal for yourself. It reminds you of why it's so important to have a plan. The best things in your life and the life you live isn't a byproduct of luck—it's the results of the choices you make. That's why excuses are not an option for you, and if they once were, forgive yourself and move forward with a "no excuse commitment" for your life. You don't want them, and you don't need them.

Your life is one big event and it's never too late to turn it around to be the way you want it to be.

At the end of each day there are two people you should want to thank for the progress you've made—God and yourself. Because of what you do together, you can create a legacy that is passed down to your kids and those around you. They don't have to have their "moment of reckoning" when they realize that something has to change in their life—that they are at their wit's end. They can grow into a healthy lifestyle that recognizes the important of exercise and food on the body, mind, and soul; that through fitness being a non-optional part of life that they are experiencing more goodness and avoiding excessive stress and uncertainty. This is awesome, and it's something *you* can do.

In a world where there are far too many "I's," this is one that is okay, because all that you want to change starts when you look into that mirror and see who you are, and then say: "I want more because ____, and I am willing to do whatever it takes to earn it through living a fit lifestyle." Because once you are uplifted, others are going to naturally be lifted up with you.

Live life in an upward and mobile manner, not a downward spiral.

Most importantly, live your life remembering that every minute counts for something, so why not make it something good.

Make it happen!

Tony

ABOUT TONY GRECO

Tony Greco is Canada's Leading Fitness Specialist and the Co-Founder of Greco Fitness (www.grecofitness.com). In the early 1990s, Tony along with his friend Paolo took a $10,000 venture loan to begin what has now grown into the leading boutique fitness gym in Canada and soon-to-be-present in the US market. Starting a business from scratch is no easy task. Everything Tony has learned about business and wellness came from passion, dedication and hard work. He doesn't give up and his record shows it. Tony won the IAKSA World Kick Boxing Championship title in 1995. In 2016, Greco Fitness merged with a team of successful Ottawa business investors and the well-established New-York based Integrity Square, an early stage growth investor in the Health, Active Lifestyle & Outdoors ("HALO") sector.

Tony is frequently sought out by some of the biggest names in the NHL. He has trained Claude Giroux (the Philadelphia Flyers), Dan Boyle (New York Rangers) and Mike Fisher (Nashville Predators), just to name a few.

Tony has also created programs for, and personally trained, Country Star Carrie Underwood and former Supermodel Carol Alt.

He is a top graduate from the Sports Performance Institute, whose certification exceeded the guidelines established by the National Fitness Leaders Advisory Council in personal training, strength training and aerobics instruction. Tony continues to go above and beyond with each and every aspect of his fitness training system, in which franchisees and clients alike, reap the benefits of an amazing program. One of the most exciting acknowledgements of his hard work was when he was awarded The Queen Elizabeth II Diamond Jubilee Medal in 2015. This is an award that is given to the Diamond Jubilee Award in 2015. This award is given by Her Majesty, Queen Elizabeth II, to individuals who have shown honorable service that helped to make their country better.

When Tony reflects on everything that happens in his life, he says, "None of this would have been possible without the determination, passion, and discipline I have set for myself." Tony's motto is: know who you are and what you want. This motto has always guided Tony through his business career, relationships, financial decisions, and health choices. His greatest hope is that it can inspire others to do the same.

CONTACT TONY

Book Tony Greco to speak
at your next event!

Contact: Felicia Pizzonia on behalf of Tony Greco
Phone:647-883-1758
E-mail: bookings@strongmindleanbody.com

Quantity discounts are available on bulk purchases of this book for reselling, educational purposes, subscription incentives, gifts, sponsorship, or fundraising. Unique books or book excerpts can also be fashioned to suit special needs such as private labeling with your logo on the cover and a message from or a message printed on the second page of the book. For more information, please contact our Special Sales Department at Ultimate Publishing House. Orders for college textbook or course adoption use.

Please contact Ultimate Publishing House Tel: 647-883-1758
or email: admin@ultimatepublishinghouse.com

RECOMMENDED RESOURCES

CHRIS LACHARITY
SALES REPRESENTATIVE

MARILYN WILSON
DREAM PROPERTIES
INC. BROKERAGE

CHRISTIE'S
INTERNATIONAL REAL ESTATE

Direct: 613-240-8609
Chris@ChrisLacharity.com

Trust is such an important factor in choosing a realtor because, if they don't have your best interests at heart throughout the entire selling process, the biggest asset you likely have will be at serious risk. Chris and his team made us feel that selling our home was their top priority. They were accessible at any time of the day or night and, with their combined wisdom and expertise in the high-end market, were wizards at achieving the best sales outcome on our behalves. These folks are the real deal in real estate and we highly recommend them to anyone who wants to be on the winning end of selling their home!

Drs Kevin and Susan Goheen

CHRIS LACHARITY

Selling Lifestyle in Ottawa for Record Value
Year After Year

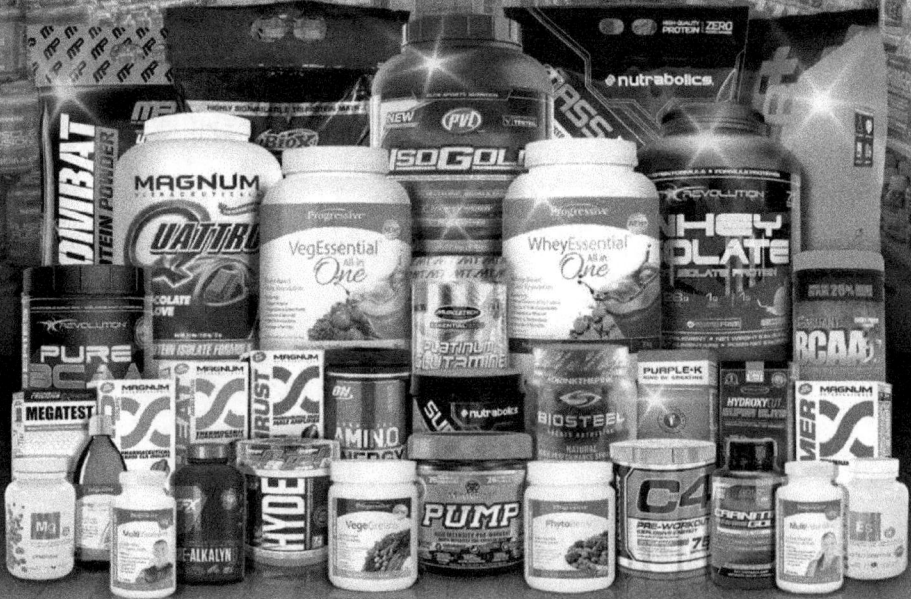

Live for today.
Plan for tomorrow.

With the right balance of life insurance
and investments, you can protect
the life you're building today, the goals
you have for tomorrow and still dream
big for the future.

**Talk to us today and discover
your financial balance.**

Home Auto Life Investments Group Business Farm Travel

the co-operators®
A Better Place For You®

Denise McLean-Paynter
Financial Advisor
McLean-Paynter & Associates Inc
202-3171 Strandherd Dr | Nepean
Phone: 613-825-1322
cooperators.ca/McLean-Paynter-Associates

GET PUBLISHED!

The Ultimate Publishing House's Production System is so precise, we can have your book released in 6 months:

All of our book publishing programs include:

- mastermind session
- personal project manager
- professional ghostwriter
- five phases of editing
- branded book website
- worldwide distribution

- marketing
- publicity
- media coaching
- book cover design
- image consulting

And much more!
UPH is here to make your book publishing dreams come true!

CALL TODAY TO START YOUR BOOK, IT IS THE BEST MARKETING INVESTMENT YOU WILL EVER MAKE!

647 883 1758 OR Email: author@ultimatepublishinghouse.com

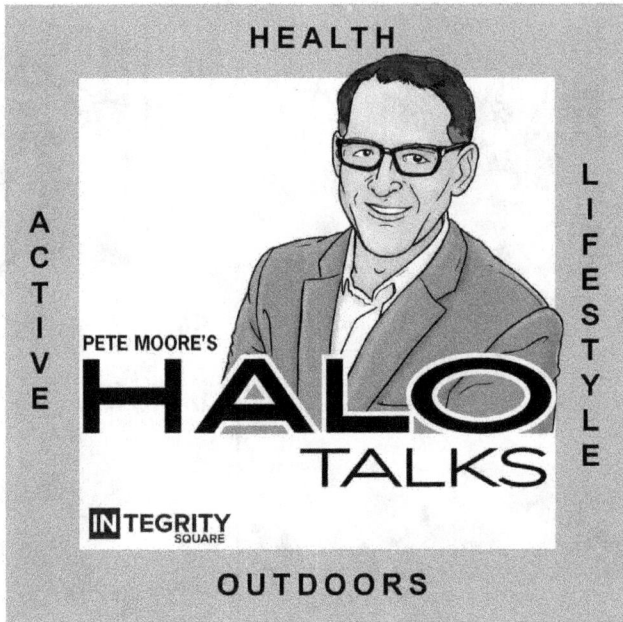

JEWELLERS

BERTUCCI DESIGN

JOAILLIERS

Westmount, Quebec, Canada
www.bertuccijewellers.com